GOOD NEWS

TOLD BY

MATTHEW

KU-365-972

This book belongs to

_____

THE BIBLE SOCIETIES

HOW TO READ THE BIBLE

PRAY ...

Ask God to help you to understand and take in the section you read.

READ ...

The Bible verses which make up this section.

THINK ...

About what you have read.

You might like to find answers to some of these questions:

What does this section teach me
about God?
about Jesus?

Is there a promise in this section?

Is there something in this section I could tell to someone else?

PRAY ...

Asking God to give you His strength to follow Jesus every day and to put into practice what you have read.

READ IT CHALLENGE

Read through the whole of Matthew's story.
Keep a record of what you have read.

1	Matthew 1: 1-25	❏	20	Matthew 10: 1-20	❏
2	Matthew 2: 1-12	❏	21	Matthew 10: 21-31	❏
3	Matthew 2: 13-23	❏	22	Matthew 10: 32-42	❏
4	Matthew 3: 1-17	❏	23	Matthew 11: 1-19	❏
5	Matthew 4: 1-11	❏	24	Matthew 11: 20-30	❏
6	Matthew 4: 12-25	❏	25	Matthew 12: 1-14	❏
7	Matthew 5: 1-12	❏	26	Matthew 12: 15-21	❏
8	Matthew 5: 13-26	❏	27	Matthew 12: 22-37	❏
9	Matthew 5: 27-37	❏	28	Matthew 12: 38-50	❏
10	Matthew 5: 38-48	❏	29	Matthew 13: 1-17	❏
11	Matthew 6: 1-15	❏	30	Matthew 13: 18-23	❏
12	Matthew 6: 16-23	❏	31	Matthew 13: 24-35	❏
13	Matthew 6: 24-34	❏	32	Matthew 13: 36-46	❏
14	Matthew 7: 1-12	❏	33	Matthew 13: 47-58	❏
15	Matthew 7: 13-29	❏	34	Matthew 14: 1-21	❏
16	Matthew 8: 1-17	❏	35	Matthew 14: 22-36	❏
17	Matthew 8: 18-34	❏	36	Matthew 15: 1-20	❏
18	Matthew 9: 1-17	❏	37	Matthew 15: 21-39	❏
19	Matthew 9: 18-38	❏	38	Matthew 16: 1-12	❏

READ IT CHALLENGE

Contents

GOOD NEWS
TOLD BY
MATTHEW

Who was Matthew?

Matthew was a tax collector who lived at the time of Jesus. Tax collectors weren't very popular then because sometimes they took extra for themselves before giving the remainder to the Romans, who ruled Jesus' homeland. Some people were surprised that people like Matthew were in Jesus' group of special friends. Matthew's life was changed through meeting Jesus and he wrote this book to provide for the people of his time a true record of what Jesus said and did.

What does he tell us about Jesus?

His account of Jesus' life is different from some biographies of famous people you might read. It doesn't tell us what Jesus looked like, nor does he go into much detail about the childhood of Jesus. Most biographies spend a lot of time describing what happens in the lifetime of their subject. Matthew spends eight of his twenty eight chapters (more than a quarter of his book) describing the events in the last week of Jesus' life. He does this because he wants us to know the facts so that we, like Matthew, can put our trust in Jesus, believe in Him and follow Him.

Outline of Contents

The Ancestors of Jesus Christ
(Lk 3.23–38)

1 This is the list of the ancestors of Jesus Christ, a descendant of David, who was a descendant of Abraham.

²⁻⁶ᵃ From Abraham to King David, the following ancestors are listed: Abraham, Isaac, Jacob, Judah and his brothers; then Perez and Zerah (their mother was Tamar), Hezron, Ram, Amminadab, Nahshon, Salmon, Boaz (his mother was Rahab), Obed (his mother was Ruth), Jesse, and King David.

⁶ᵇ⁻¹¹ From David to the time when the people of Israel were taken into exile in Babylon, the following ancestors are listed: David, Solomon (his mother was the woman who had been Uriah's wife), Rehoboam, Abijah, Asa, Jehoshaphat, Jehoram, Uzziah, Jotham, Ahaz, Hezekiah, Manasseh, Amon, Josiah, and Jehoiachin and his brothers.

¹²⁻¹⁶ From the time after the exile in Babylon to the birth of Jesus, the following ancestors are listed: Jehoiachin, Shealtiel, Zerubbabel, Abiud, Eliakim, Azor, Zadok, Achim, Eliud, Eleazar, Matthan, Jacob, and Joseph, who married Mary, the mother of Jesus, who was called the Messiah.

¹⁷ So then, there were fourteen generations from Abraham to David, and fourteen from David to the exile in Babylon, and fourteen from then to the birth of the Messiah.

The Birth of Jesus Christ
(Lk 2.1–7)

18 This was how the birth of Jesus Christ took place. His mother Mary was engaged to Joseph, but before they were married, she found out that she was going to have a baby by the Holy Spirit. 19 Joseph was a man who always did what was right, but he did not want to disgrace Mary publicly; so he made plans to break the engagement privately. 20 While he was thinking about this, an angel of the Lord appeared to him in a dream and said, "Joseph, descendant of David, do not be afraid to take Mary to be your wife. For it is by the Holy Spirit that she has conceived. 21 She will have a son, and you will name him Jesus — because he will save his people from their sins."

22 Now all this happened in order to make what the Lord had said through the prophet come true, 23 "A virgin will become pregnant and have a son, and he will be called Immanuel" (which means, "God is with us").

24 So when Joseph woke up, he married Mary, as the angel of the Lord had told him to do. 25 But he had no sexual relations with her before she gave birth to her son. And Joseph named him Jesus.

Visitors from the East

2 Jesus was born in the town of Bethlehem in Judea, during the time when Herod was king. Soon afterwards, some men who studied the stars came from the east to Jerusalem 2 and asked, "Where is the baby born to be the king of the Jews? We saw his star when it came up in the east, and we have come to worship him."

3 When King Herod heard about this, he was very upset, and so was everyone else in Jerusalem. 4 He called together all the chief priests and the teachers of the Law and asked them, "Where will the Messiah be born?"

5 "In the town of Bethlehem in Judea," they answered. "For this is what the prophet wrote:

6 'Bethlehem in the land of Judah,
    you are by no means the least of the leading cities of Judah;
  for from you will come a leader
    who will guide my people Israel.' "

⁷ So Herod called the visitors from the east to a secret meeting and found out from them the exact time the star had appeared. ⁸ Then he sent them to Bethlehem with these instructions: "Go and make a careful search for the child, and when you find him, let me know, so that I too may go and worship him."

⁹⁻¹⁰ And so they left, and on their way they saw the same star they had seen in the east. When they saw it, how happy they were, what joy was theirs! It went ahead of them until it stopped over the place where the child was. ¹¹ They went into the house, and when they saw the child with his mother Mary, they knelt down and worshipped him. They brought out their gifts of gold, frankincense, and myrrh, and presented them to him.

The same star . . . went ahead of them   (2.9-10)

¹² Then they returned to their country by another road, since God had warned them in a dream not to go back to Herod.

The Escape to Egypt

¹³ After they had left, an angel of the Lord appeared in a dream to Joseph and said, "Herod will be looking for the child in order to kill him. So get up, take the child and his mother and escape to Egypt, and stay there until I tell you to leave."

¹⁴Joseph got up, took the child and his mother, and left during the night for Egypt, ¹⁵where he stayed until Herod died. This was done to make what the Lord had said through the prophet come true, "I called my Son out of Egypt."

The Killing of the Children

¹⁶When Herod realized that the visitors from the east had tricked him, he was furious. He gave orders to kill all the boys in Bethlehem and its neighbourhood who were two years old and younger — this was done in accordance with what he had learned from the visitors about the time when the star had appeared.

¹⁷In this way what the prophet Jeremiah had said came true:

¹⁸ "A sound is heard in Ramah,
     the sound of bitter weeping.
   Rachel is crying for her children;
     she refuses to be comforted,
     for they are dead."

The Return from Egypt

¹⁹After Herod died, an angel of the Lord appeared in a dream to Joseph in Egypt ²⁰and said, "Get up, take the child and his mother, and go back to the land of Israel, because those who tried to kill the child are dead." ²¹So Joseph got up, took the child and his mother, and went back to Israel.

²²But when Joseph heard that Archelaus had succeeded his father Herod as king of Judea, he was afraid to go there. He was given more instructions in a dream, so he went to the province of Galilee ²³and made his home in a town named Nazareth. And so what the prophets had said came true: "He will be called a Nazarene."

The Preaching of John the Baptist
(Mk 1.1–8; Lk 3.1–18; Jn 1.19–28)

3 At that time John the Baptist came to the desert of Judea and started preaching. ²"Turn away from your sins," he said, "because the Kingdom of heaven is near!" ³John was the man the prophet Isaiah was talking about when he said:

"Someone is shouting in the desert,
  'Prepare a road for the Lord;
  make a straight path for him to travel!' "

⁴John's clothes were made of camel's hair; he wore a leather belt round his waist, and his food was locusts and wild honey. ⁵People came to him from Jerusalem, from the whole province of Judea, and from all the country near the River Jordan. ⁶They confessed their sins, and he baptized them in the Jordan.

⁷When John saw many Pharisees and Sadducees coming to him to be baptized, he said to them, "You snakes — who told you that you could escape from the punishment God is about to send? ⁸Do those things that will show that you have turned from your sins. ⁹And don't think you can escape punishment by saying that Abraham is your ancestor. I tell you that God can take these stones and make descendants for Abraham! ¹⁰The axe is ready to cut down the trees at the roots; every tree that does not bear good fruit will be cut down and thrown in the fire. ¹¹I baptize you with water to show that you have repented, but the one who will come after me will baptize you with the Holy Spirit and fire. He is much greater than I am; and I am not good enough even to carry his sandals. ¹²He has his winnowing shovel with him to thresh out all the grain. He will gather his wheat into his barn, but he will burn the chaff in a fire that never goes out."

The Baptism of Jesus
(Mk 1.9–11; Lk 3.21–22)

¹³At that time Jesus arrived from Galilee and came to John at the Jordan to be baptized by him. ¹⁴But John tried to make him change his mind. "I ought to be baptized by you," John said, "and yet you have come to me!"

¹⁵But Jesus answered him, "Let it be so for now. For in this way we shall do all that God requires." So John agreed.

¹⁶As soon as Jesus was baptized, he came up out of the water. Then heaven was opened to him, and he saw the Spirit of God coming down like a dove and alighting on him. ¹⁷Then a voice said from heaven, "This is my own dear Son, with whom I am pleased."

The Temptation of Jesus
(Mk 1.12–13; Lk 4.1–13)

4 Then the Spirit led Jesus into the desert to be tempted by the Devil. ²After spending 40 days and nights without food, Jesus was hungry. ³Then the Devil came to him and said, "If you are God's Son, order these stones to turn into bread."

Then the Spirit led Jesus into the desert ... (4.1)

⁴But Jesus answered, "The scripture says, 'Human beings cannot live on bread alone, but need every word that God speaks.' "

⁵Then the Devil took Jesus to Jerusalem, the Holy City, set him on the highest point of the Temple, ⁶and said to him, "If you are God's Son, throw yourself down, for the scripture says:
  'God will give orders to his angels about you;
    they will hold you up with their hands,
    so that not even your feet will be hurt on the stones.' "

⁷Jesus answered, "But the scripture also says, 'Do not put the Lord your God to the test.' "

⁸Then the Devil took Jesus to a very high mountain and showed him all the kingdoms of the world in all their greatness. ⁹ "All this I will give you," the Devil said, "if you kneel down and worship me."

¹⁰Then Jesus answered, "Go away, Satan! The scripture says, 'Worship the Lord your God and serve only him!' "

¹¹Then the Devil left Jesus; and angels came and helped him.

Jesus Begins his Work in Galilee
(Mk 1.14–15; Lk 4.14–15)

¹²When Jesus heard that John had been put in prison, he went away to Galilee. ¹³He did not stay in Nazareth, but went to live in Capernaum, a town by Lake Galilee, in the territory of Zebulun and Naphtali. ¹⁴This was done to make what the prophet Isaiah had said come true:

¹⁵ "Land of Zebulun and land of Naphtali,
    on the road to the sea, on the other side of the Jordan,
    Galilee, land of the Gentiles!
¹⁶ The people who live in darkness
    will see a great light.
  On those who live in the dark land of death
    the light will shine."

¹⁷From that time Jesus began to preach his message: "Turn away from your sins, because the Kingdom of heaven is near!"

Jesus Calls Four Fishermen
(Mk 1.16–20; Lk 5.1–11)

¹⁸As Jesus walked along the shore of Lake Galilee, he saw two brothers who were fishermen, Simon (called Peter) and his brother Andrew, catching fish in the lake with a net. ¹⁹Jesus said to them, "Come with me, and I will teach you to catch people." ²⁰At once they left their nets and went with him.

²¹He went on and saw two other brothers, James and John, the sons of Zebedee. They were in their boat with their father Zebedee, getting their nets ready. Jesus called them, ²²and at once they left the boat and their father, and went with him.

Jesus Teaches, Preaches, and Heals
(Lk 6.17–19)

²³ Jesus went all over Galilee, teaching in the synagogues, preaching the Good News about the Kingdom, and healing people who had all kinds of disease and sickness. ²⁴ The news about him spread through the whole country of Syria, so that people brought to him all those who were sick, suffering from all kinds of diseases and disorders: people with demons, and epileptics, and paralytics — and Jesus healed them all. ²⁵ Large crowds followed him from Galilee and the Ten Towns, from Jerusalem, Judea, and the land on the other side of the Jordan.

THE SERMON ON THE MOUNT
5.1—7.29

5 Jesus saw the crowds and went up a hill, where he sat down. His disciples gathered round him, ² and he began to teach them:

True Happiness
(Lk 6.20–23)

³ "Happy are those who know they are spiritually poor;
  the Kingdom of heaven belongs to them!
⁴ Happy are those who mourn;
  God will comfort them!
⁵ Happy are those who are humble;
  they will receive what God has promised!
⁶ Happy are those whose greatest desire is to do what
    God requires;
  God will satisfy them fully!
⁷ Happy are those who are merciful to others;
  God will be merciful to them!
⁸ Happy are the pure in heart;
  they will see God!
⁹ Happy are those who work for peace;
  God will call them his children!
¹⁰ Happy are those who are persecuted because they do
    what God requires;
  the Kingdom of heaven belongs to them!
¹¹ "Happy are you when people insult you and persecute you and tell all kinds of evil lies against you because you are

my followers. [12] Be happy and glad, for a great reward is kept for you in heaven. This is how the prophets who lived before you were persecuted.

Salt and Light
(Mk 9.50; Lk 14.34–35)

[13] "You are like salt for the whole human race. But if salt loses its saltiness, there is no way to make it salty again. It has become worthless, so it is thrown out and people trample on it.

[14] "You are like light for the whole world. A city built on a hill cannot be hidden. [15] No one lights a lamp and puts it under a bowl; instead he puts it on the lampstand, where it gives light for everyone in the house. [16] In the same way your light must shine before people, so that they will see the good things you do and praise your Father in heaven.

Teaching about the Law

[17] "Do not think that I have come to do away with the Law of Moses and the teachings of the prophets. I have not come to do away with them, but to make their teachings come true. [18] Remember that as long as heaven and earth last, not the least point nor the smallest detail of the Law will be done away with — not until the end of all things. [a] [19] So then, whoever disobeys even the least important of the commandments and teaches others to do the same, will be least in the Kingdom of heaven. On the other hand, whoever obeys the Law and teaches others to do the same, will be great in the Kingdom of heaven. [20] I tell you, then, that you will be able to enter the Kingdom of heaven only if you are more faithful than the teachers of the Law and the Pharisees in doing what God requires.

Teaching about Anger
(Lk 12.57–59)

[21] "You have heard that people were told in the past, 'Do not commit murder; anyone who does will be brought to trial.' [22] But now I tell you: whoever is angry[b] with his

a **5.18** the end of all things; *or* all its teachings come true.
b **5.22** whoever is angry; *some manuscripts have* whoever without cause is angry.

brother will be brought to trial, whoever calls his brother 'You good-for-nothing!' will be brought before the Council, and whoever calls his brother a worthless fool will be in danger of going to the fire of hell. ²³ So if you are about to offer your gift to God at the altar and there you remember that your brother has something against you, ²⁴ leave your gift there in front of the altar, go at once and make peace with your brother, and then come back and offer your gift to God.

²⁵ "If someone brings a lawsuit against you and takes you to court, settle the dispute with him while there is time, before you get to court. Once you are there, he will hand you over to the judge, who will hand you over to the police, and you will be put in jail. ²⁶ There you will stay, I tell you, until you pay the last penny of your fine.

Teaching about Adultery

²⁷ "You have heard that it was said, 'Do not commit adultery.' ²⁸ But now I tell you: anyone who looks at a woman and wants to possess her is guilty of committing adultery with her in his heart. ²⁹ So if your right eye causes you to sin, take it out and throw it away! It is much better for you to lose a part of your body than to have your whole body thrown into hell. ³⁰ If your right hand causes you to sin, cut it off and throw it away! It is much better for you to lose one of your limbs than for your whole body to go to hell.

Teaching about Divorce
(Mt 19.9; Mk 10.11–12; Lk 16.18)

³¹ "It was also said, 'Anyone who divorces his wife must give her a written notice of divorce.' ³² But now I tell you: if a man divorces his wife, for any cause other than her unfaithfulness, then he is guilty of making her commit adultery if she marries again; and the man who marries her commits adultery also.

Teaching about Vows

³³ "You have also heard that people were told in the past, 'Do not break your promise, but do what you have vowed to the Lord to do.' ³⁴ But now I tell you: do not use any vow when you make a promise. Do not swear by heaven, for it is God's

throne; [35] nor by earth, for it is the resting place for his feet; nor by Jerusalem, for it is the city of the great King. [36] Do not even swear by your head, because you cannot make a single hair white or black. [37] Just say 'Yes' or 'No' — anything else you say comes from the Evil One.

Teaching about Revenge
(Lk 6.29–30)

[38] "You have heard that it was said, 'An eye for an eye, and a tooth for a tooth.' [39] But now I tell you: do not take revenge on someone who wrongs you. If anyone slaps you on the right cheek, let him slap your left cheek too. [40] And if someone takes you to court to sue you for your shirt, let him have your coat as well. [41] And if one of the occupation troops forces you to carry his pack one kilometre, carry it two kilometres. [42] When someone asks you for something, give it to him; when someone wants to borrow something, lend it to him.

Love for Enemies
(Lk 6.27–28, 32–36)

[43] "You have heard that it was said, 'Love your friends, hate your enemies.' [44] But now I tell you: love your enemies and pray for those who persecute you, [45] so that you may become the children of your Father in heaven. For he makes his sun to shine on bad and good people alike, and gives rain to those who do good and to those who do evil. [46] Why should God reward you if you love only the people who love you? Even the tax collectors do that! [47] And if you speak only to your friends, have you done anything out of the ordinary? Even the pagans do that! [48] You must be perfect — just as your Father in heaven is perfect!

Teaching about Charity

6 "Make certain you do not perform your religious duties in public so that people will see what you do. If you do these things publicly, you will not have any reward from your Father in heaven.

[2] "So when you give something to a needy person, do not make a big show of it, as the hypocrites do in the houses of worship and on the streets. They do it so that people will praise

When you help a needy person ...   (6.3)

them. I assure you, they have already been paid in full. ³But when you help a needy person, do it in such a way that even your closest friend will not know about it. ⁴Then it will be a private matter. And your Father, who sees what you do in private, will reward you.

Teaching about Prayer
(Lk 11.2–4)

⁵ "When you pray, do not be like the hypocrites! They love to stand up and pray in the houses of worship and on the street corners, so that everyone will see them. I assure you, they have already been paid in full. ⁶But when you pray, go to your room, close the door, and pray to your Father, who is unseen. And your Father, who sees what you do in private, will reward you.

⁷ "When you pray, do not use a lot of meaningless words, as the pagans do, who think that their gods will hear them because their prayers are long. ⁸Do not be like them. Your Father already knows what you need before you ask him. ⁹This, then, is how you should pray:

'Our Father in heaven:
  May your holy name be honoured;
10   may your Kingdom come;
  may your will be done on earth as it is in heaven.
11   Give us today the food we need. [a]
12   Forgive us the wrongs we have done,
  as we forgive the wrongs that others have done to us.
13   Do not bring us to hard testing,
  but keep us safe from the Evil One.' [b]

14 "If you forgive others the wrongs they have done to you, your Father in heaven will also forgive you. 15 But if you do not forgive others, then your Father will not forgive the wrongs you have done.

Teaching about Fasting

16 "And when you fast, do not put on a sad face as the hypocrites do. They neglect their appearance so that everyone will see that they are fasting. I assure you, they have already been paid in full. 17 When you go without food, wash your face and comb your hair, 18 so that others cannot know that you are fasting — only your Father, who is unseen, will know. And your Father, who sees what you do in private, will reward you.

Riches in Heaven
(Lk 12.33–34)

19 "Do not store up riches for yourselves here on earth, where moths and rust destroy, and robbers break in and steal. 20 Instead, store up riches for yourselves in heaven, where moths and rust cannot destroy, and robbers cannot break in and steal. 21 For your heart will always be where your riches are.

The Light of the Body
(Lk 11.34–36)

22 "The eyes are like a lamp for the body. If your eyes are sound, your whole body will be full of light; 23 but if your eyes are no good, your body will be in darkness. So if the light in you is darkness, how terribly dark it will be!

a **6.11** we need; *or* for today; *or* for tomorrow.
b **6.13** *Some manuscripts add* For yours is the kingdom, and the power, and the glory for ever. Amen.

God and Possessions
(Lk 16.13; 12.22–31)

²⁴ "No one can be a slave of two masters; he will hate one and love the other; he will be loyal to one and despise the other. You cannot serve both God and money.

²⁵ "This is why I tell you not to be worried about the food and drink you need in order to stay alive, or about clothes for your body. After all, isn't life worth more than food? And isn't the body worth more than clothes? ²⁶ Look at the birds: they do not sow seeds, gather a harvest and put it in barns; yet your Father in heaven takes care of them! Aren't you worth much more than birds? ²⁷ Can any of you live a bit longer[a] by worrying about it?

Look how the wild flowers grow ...   (6.28)

²⁸ "And why worry about clothes? Look how the wild flowers grow: they do not work or make clothes for themselves. ²⁹ But I tell you that not even King Solomon with all his wealth had clothes as beautiful as one of these flowers. ³⁰ It is God who clothes the wild grass — grass that is here today and gone tomorrow, burnt up in the oven. Won't he be all the more sure to clothe you? How little faith you have!

³¹ "So do not start worrying: 'Where will my food come from? or my drink? or my clothes?' ³² (These are the things

a **6.27** live a bit longer; *or* grow a bit taller.

the pagans are always concerned about.) Your Father in
heaven knows that you need all these things. ³³ Instead, be
concerned above everything else with the Kingdom of God
and with what he requires of you, and he will provide you with
all these other things. ³⁴ So do not worry about tomorrow; it
will have enough worries of its own. There is no need to add
to the troubles each day brings.

Judging Others
(Lk 6.37–38, 41–42)

7 "Do not judge others, so that God will not judge you,
²for God will judge you in the same way as you judge
others, and he will apply to you the same rules you apply
to others. ³ Why, then, do you look at the speck in your
brother's eye, and pay no attention to the log in your own
eye? ⁴ How dare you say to your brother, 'Please, let me take
that speck out of your eye,' when you have a log in your own
eye? ⁵ You hypocrite! First take the log out of your own eye,
and then you will be able to see clearly to take the speck out
of your brother's eye.

⁶ "Do not give what is holy to dogs — they will only turn
and attack you. Do not throw your pearls in front of pigs —
they will only trample them underfoot.

Ask, Seek, Knock
(Lk 11.9–13)

⁷ "Ask, and you will receive; seek, and you will find; knock,
and the door will be opened to you. ⁸ For everyone who asks
will receive, and anyone who seeks will find, and the door will
be opened to those who knock. ⁹ Would any of you who
are fathers give your son a stone when he asks for bread?
¹⁰ Or would you give him a snake when he asks for a fish?
¹¹ Bad as you are, you know how to give good things to your
children. How much more, then, will your Father in heaven
give good things to those who ask him!

¹² "Do for others what you want them to do for you: this
is the meaning of the Law of Moses and of the teachings of
the prophets.

The Narrow Gate
(Lk 13.24)

[13] "Go in through the narrow gate, because the gate to hell is wide and the road that leads to it is easy, and there are many who travel it. [14] But the gate to life is narrow and the way that leads to it is hard, and there are few people who find it.

A Tree and its Fruit
(Lk 6.43–44)

[15] "Be on your guard against false prophets; they come to you looking like sheep on the outside, but on the inside they are really like wild wolves. [16] You will know them by what they do. Thorn bushes do not bear grapes, and briars do not bear figs. [17] A healthy tree bears good fruit, but a poor tree bears bad fruit. [18] A healthy tree cannot bear bad fruit, and a poor tree cannot bear good fruit. [19] And any tree that does not bear good fruit is cut down and thrown in the fire. [20] So then, you will know the false prophets by what they do.

I Never Knew You
(Lk 13.25–27)

[21] "Not everyone who calls me 'Lord, Lord' will enter the Kingdom of heaven, but only those who do what my Father in heaven wants them to do. [22] When Judgement Day comes, many will say to me, 'Lord, Lord! In your name we spoke God's message, by your name we drove out many demons and performed many miracles!' [23] Then I will say to them, 'I never knew you. Get away from me, you wicked people!'

The Two House Builders
(Lk 6.47–49)

[24] "So then, anyone who hears these words of mine and obeys them is like a wise man who built his house on rock. [25] The rain poured down, the rivers overflowed, and the wind blew hard against that house. But it did not fall, because it was built on rock.

[26] "But anyone who hears these words of mine and does not obey them is like a foolish man who built his house on

sand. [27] The rain poured down, the rivers overflowed, the wind blew hard against that house, and it fell. And what a terrible fall that was!"

The Authority of Jesus

[28] When Jesus finished saying these things, the crowd was amazed at the way he taught. [29] He wasn't like the teachers of the Law; instead, he taught with authority.

Jesus Heals a Man
(Mk 1.40–45; Lk 5.12–16)

8 When Jesus came down from the hill, large crowds followed him. [2] Then a man suffering from a dreaded skin disease came to him, knelt down before him, and said, "Sir, if you want to, you can make me clean." [a]

[3] Jesus stretched out his hand and touched him. "I do want to," he answered. "Be clean!" At once the man was healed of his disease. [4] Then Jesus said to him, "Listen! Don't tell anyone, but go straight to the priest and let him examine you; then in order to prove to everyone that you are cured, offer the sacrifice that Moses ordered."

Jesus Heals a Roman Officer's Servant
(Lk 7.1–10)

[5] When Jesus entered Capernaum, a Roman officer met him and begged for help: [6] "Sir, my servant is sick in bed at home, unable to move and suffering terribly."

[7] "I will go and make him well," Jesus said.

[8] "Oh no, sir," answered the officer. "I do not deserve to have you come into my house. Just give the order, and my servant will get well. [9] I, too, am a man under the authority of superior officers, and I have soldiers under me. I order this one, 'Go!' and he goes; and I order that one, 'Come!' and he comes; and I order my slave, 'Do this!' and he does it."

[10] When Jesus heard this, he was surprised and said to the people following him, "I tell you, I have never found anyone in Israel with faith like this. [11] I assure you that many will come from the east and the west and sit down with Abraham, Isaac,

a **8.2** MAKE ME CLEAN: *This disease was considered to make a person ritually unclean.*

and Jacob at the feast in the Kingdom of heaven. [12]But those who should be in the Kingdom will be thrown out into the darkness, where they will cry and grind their teeth." [13]Then Jesus said to the officer, "Go home, and what you believe will be done for you."

And the officer's servant was healed that very moment.

Jesus Heals Many People
(Mk 1.29–34; Lk 4.38–41)

[14]Jesus went to Peter's home, and there he saw Peter's mother-in-law sick in bed with a fever. [15]He touched her hand; the fever left her, and she got up and began to wait on him.

[16]When evening came, people brought to Jesus many who had demons in them. Jesus drove out the evil spirits with a word and healed all who were sick. [17]He did this to make what the prophet Isaiah had said come true, "He himself took our sickness and carried away our diseases."

The Would-be Followers of Jesus
(Lk 9.57–62)

[18]When Jesus noticed the crowd round him, he ordered his disciples to go to the other side of the lake. [19]A teacher of the Law came to him. "Teacher," he said, "I am ready to go with you wherever you go."

[20]Jesus answered him, "Foxes have holes, and birds have nests, but the Son of Man has nowhere to lie down and rest."

[21]Another man, who was a disciple, said, "Sir, first let me go back and bury my father."

[22]"Follow me," Jesus answered, "and let the dead bury their own dead."

Jesus Calms a Storm
(Mk 4.35–41; Lk 8.22–25)

[23]Jesus got into a boat, and his disciples went with him. [24]Suddenly a fierce storm hit the lake, and the boat was in danger of sinking. But Jesus was asleep. [25]The disciples went to him and woke him up. "Save us, Lord!" they said. "We are about to die!"

²⁶ "Why are you so frightened?" Jesus answered. "How little faith you have!" Then he got up and ordered the winds and the waves to stop, and there was a great calm.

²⁷ Everyone was amazed. "What kind of man is this?" they said. "Even the winds and the waves obey him!"

Jesus Heals Two Men with Demons
(Mk 5.1–20; Lk 8.26–39)

²⁸ When Jesus came to the territory of Gadara on the other side of the lake, he was met by two men who came out of the burial caves there. These men had demons in them and were so fierce that no one dared travel on that road. ²⁹ At once they screamed, "What do you want with us, you Son of God? Have you come to punish us before the right time?"

³⁰ Not far away there was a large herd of pigs feeding. ³¹ So the demons begged Jesus, "If you are going to drive us out, send us into that herd of pigs."

³² "Go," Jesus told them; so they left and went off into the pigs. The whole herd rushed down the side of the cliff into the lake and was drowned.

³³ The men who had been taking care of the pigs ran away and went into the town, where they told the whole story and what had happened to the men with the demons. ³⁴ So everyone from the town went out to meet Jesus; and when they saw him, they begged him to leave their territory.

Jesus Heals a Paralysed Man
(Mk 2.1–12; Lk 5.17–26)

9 Jesus got into the boat and went back across the lake to his own town,ᵃ ²where some people brought to him a paralysed man, lying on a bed. When Jesus saw how much faith they had, he said to the paralysed man, "Courage, my son! Your sins are forgiven."

³ Then some teachers of the Law said to themselves, "This man is speaking blasphemy!"

⁴ Jesus perceived what they were thinking, so he said, "Why are you thinking such evil things? ⁵ Is it easier to say, 'Your sins are forgiven,' or to say, 'Get up and walk'? ⁶ I will

a **9.1** HIS OWN TOWN: *Capernaum (see 4.13).*

prove to you, then, that the Son of Man has authority on earth to forgive sins." So he said to the paralysed man, "Get up, pick up your bed, and go home!"

[7] The man got up and went home. [8] When the people saw it, they were afraid, and praised God for giving such authority to people.

Jesus Calls Matthew
(Mk 2.13–17; Lk 5.27–32)

[9] Jesus left that place, and as he walked along, he saw a tax collector, named Matthew, sitting in his office. He said to him, "Follow me."

Matthew got up and followed him.

[10] While Jesus was having a meal in Matthew's house,[a] many tax collectors and other outcasts came and joined Jesus and his disciples at the table. [11] Some Pharisees saw this and asked his disciples, "Why does your teacher eat with such people?"

[12] Jesus heard them and answered, "People who are well do not need a doctor, but only those who are sick. [13] Go and find out what is meant by the scripture that says: 'It is kindness that I want, not animal sacrifices.' I have not come to call respectable people, but outcasts."

The Question about Fasting
(Mk 2.18–22; Lk 5.33–39)

[14] Then the followers of John the Baptist came to Jesus, asking, "Why is it that we and the Pharisees fast often, but your disciples don't fast at all?"

[15] Jesus answered, "Do you expect the guests at a wedding party to be sad as long as the bridegroom is with them? Of course not! But the day will come when the bridegroom will be taken away from them, and then they will fast.

[16] "No one patches up an old coat with a piece of new cloth, for the new patch will shrink and make an even bigger hole in the coat. [17] Nor does anyone pour new wine into used wineskins, for the skins will burst, the wine will pour out, and the skins will be ruined. Instead, new wine is poured into fresh wineskins, and both will keep in good condition."

a **9.10** in Matthew's house; *or* in his (*that is,* Jesus') house.

The Official's Daughter and the Woman who Touched Jesus' Cloak
(Mk 5.21–43; Lk 8.40–56)

¹⁸While Jesus was saying this, a Jewish official came to him, knelt down before him, and said, "My daughter has just died; but come and place your hands on her, and she will live."

¹⁹So Jesus got up and followed him, and his disciples went along with him.

²⁰A woman who had suffered from severe bleeding for twelve years came up behind Jesus and touched the edge of his cloak. ²¹She said to herself, "If I only touch his cloak, I will get well."

Jesus touches lives today.

²²Jesus turned round and saw her, and said, "Courage, my daughter! Your faith has made you well." At that very moment the woman became well.

²³Then Jesus went into the official's house. When he saw the musicians for the funeral and the people all stirred up, ²⁴he said, "Get out, everybody! The little girl is not dead — she is only sleeping!" Then they all laughed at him. ²⁵But as soon as the people had been put out, Jesus went into the girl's room and took hold of her hand, and she got up. ²⁶The news about this spread all over that part of the country.

Jesus Heals Two Blind Men

²⁷Jesus left that place, and as he walked along, two blind men started following him. "Take pity on us, Son of David!" they shouted.

²⁸When Jesus had gone indoors, the two blind men came to him, and he asked them, "Do you believe that I can heal you?"

"Yes, sir!" they answered.

²⁹Then Jesus touched their eyes and said, "Let it happen, then, just as you believe!" — ³⁰and their sight was restored. Jesus spoke sternly to them, "Don't tell this to anyone!"

³¹But they left and spread the news about Jesus all over that part of the country.

Jesus Heals a Man who could not Speak

³²As the men were leaving, some people brought to Jesus a man who could not talk because he had a demon. ³³But as soon as the demon was driven out, the man started talking, and everyone was amazed. "We have never seen anything like this in Israel!" they exclaimed.

³⁴But the Pharisees said, "It is the chief of the demons who gives Jesus the power to drive out demons."

Jesus has Pity for the People

³⁵Jesus went round visiting all the towns and villages. He taught in the synagogues, preached the Good News about the Kingdom, and healed people with every kind of disease and sickness. ³⁶As he saw the crowds, his heart was filled with pity for them, because they were worried and helpless, like sheep without a shepherd. ³⁷So he said to his disciples, "The harvest is large, but there are few workers to gather it in. ³⁸Pray to the owner of the harvest that he will send out workers to gather in his harvest."

The Twelve Apostles
(Mk 3.13–19; Lk 6.12–16)

10 Jesus called his twelve disciples together and gave them authority to drive out evil spirits and to heal every disease and every sickness. ²These are the names of the twelve apostles: first, Simon (called Peter) and his

brother Andrew; James and his brother John, the sons of Zebedee; [3] Philip and Bartholomew; Thomas and Matthew, the tax collector; James son of Alphaeus, and Thaddaeus; [4] Simon the Patriot, and Judas Iscariot, who betrayed Jesus.

The Mission of the Twelve
(Mk 6.7–13; Lk 9.1–6)

[5] These twelve men were sent out by Jesus with the following instructions: "Do not go to any Gentile territory or any Samaritan towns. [6] Instead, you are to go to the lost sheep of the people of Israel. [7] Go and preach, 'The Kingdom of heaven is near!' [8] Heal the sick, bring the dead back to life, heal those who suffer from dreaded skin diseases, and drive out demons. You have received without paying, so give without being paid. [9] Do not carry any gold, silver, or copper money in your pockets; [10] do not carry a beggar's bag for the journey or an extra shirt or shoes or a stick. Workers should be given what they need.

[11] "When you come to a town or village, go in and look for someone who is willing to welcome you, and stay with him until you leave that place. [12] When you go into a house, say, 'Peace be with you.' [13] If the people in that house welcome you, let your greeting of peace remain; but if they do not welcome you, then take back your greeting. [14] And if some home or town will not welcome you or listen to you, then leave that place and shake the dust off your feet. [15] I assure you that on the Judgement Day God will show more mercy to the people of Sodom and Gomorrah than to the people of that town!

Coming Persecutions
(Mk 13.9–13; Lk 21.12–17)

[16] "Listen! I am sending you out just like sheep to a pack of wolves. You must be as cautious as snakes and as gentle as doves. [17] Watch out, for there will be those who will arrest you and take you to court, and they will whip you in the synagogues. [18] For my sake you will be brought to trial before rulers and kings, to tell the Good News to them and to the Gentiles. [19] When they bring you to trial, do not worry about what you are going to say or how you will say it; when the

time comes, you will be given what you will say. [20] For the words you will speak will not be yours; they will come from the Spirit of your Father speaking through you.

[21] "Men will hand over their own brothers to be put to death, and fathers will do the same to their children; children will turn against their parents and have them put to death. [22] Everyone will hate you because of me. But whoever holds out to the end will be saved. [23] When they persecute you in one town, run away to another one. I assure you that you will not finish your work in all the towns of Israel before the Son of Man comes.

[24] "No pupil is greater than his teacher; no slave is greater than his master. [25] So a pupil should be satisfied to become like his teacher, and a slave like his master. If the head of the family is called Beelzebul, the members of the family will be called even worse names!

Whom to Fear
(Lk 12.2-7)

[26] "So do not be afraid of people. Whatever is now covered up will be uncovered, and every secret will be made known. [27] What I am telling you in the dark you must repeat in broad daylight, and what you have heard in private you must announce from the housetops. [28] Do not be afraid of those who kill the body but cannot kill the soul; rather be afraid of God, who can destroy both body and soul in hell. [29] For only a penny you can buy two sparrows, yet not one sparrow falls to the ground without your Father's consent. [30] As for you, even the hairs of your head have all been counted. [31] So do not be afraid; you are worth much more than many sparrows!

Confessing and Rejecting Christ
(Lk 12.8-9)

[32] "For those who declare publicly that they belong to me, I will do the same before my Father in heaven. [33] But if anyone rejects me publicly, I will reject him before my Father in heaven.

Not Peace, but a Sword
(Lk 12.51–53; 14.26–27)

³⁴ "Do not think that I have come to bring peace to the world. No, I did not come to bring peace, but a sword. ³⁵ I came to set sons against their fathers, daughters against their mothers, daughters-in-law against their mothers-in-law; ³⁶ your worst enemies will be the members of your own family.

³⁷ "Those who love their father or mother more than me are not fit to be my disciples; those who love their son or daughter more than me are not fit to be my disciples. ³⁸ Those who do not take up their cross and follow in my steps are not fit to be my disciples. ³⁹ Those who try to gain their own life will lose it; but those who lose their life for my sake will gain it.

Rewards
(Mk 9.41)

⁴⁰ "Whoever welcomes you welcomes me; and whoever welcomes me welcomes the one who sent me. ⁴¹ Whoever welcomes God's messenger because he is God's messenger, will share in his reward. And whoever welcomes a good man because he is good, will share in his reward. ⁴² You can be sure that whoever gives even a drink of cold water to one of the least of these my followers because he is my follower, will certainly receive a reward."

The Messengers from John the Baptist
(Lk 7.18–35)

11 When Jesus finished giving these instructions to his twelve disciples, he left that place and went off to teach and preach in the towns near there.

² When John the Baptist heard in prison about the things that Christ was doing, he sent some of his disciples to him. ³ "Tell us," they asked Jesus, "are you the one John said was going to come, or should we expect someone else?"

⁴ Jesus answered, "Go back and tell John what you are hearing and seeing: ⁵ the blind can see, the lame can walk, those who suffer from dreaded skin diseases are made clean, ᵃ the deaf hear, the dead are brought back to life,

a **11.5** MADE CLEAN: *See 8.2.*

and the Good News is preached to the poor. [6] How happy are those who have no doubts about me!"

[7] While John's disciples were leaving, Jesus spoke about him to the crowds: "When you went out to John in the desert, what did you expect to see? A blade of grass bending in the wind? [8] What did you go out to see? A man dressed up in fancy clothes? People who dress like that live in palaces! [9] Tell me, what did you go out to see? A prophet? Yes indeed, but you saw much more than a prophet. [10] For John is the one of whom the scripture says: 'God said, I will send my messenger ahead of you to open the way for you.' [11] I assure you that John the Baptist is greater than anyone who has ever lived. But the one who is least in the Kingdom of heaven is greater than John. [12] From the time John preached his message until this very day the Kingdom of heaven has suffered violent attacks,[a] and violent men try to seize it. [13] Until the time of John all the prophets and the Law of Moses spoke about the Kingdom; [14] and if you are willing to believe their message, John is Elijah, whose coming was predicted. [15] Listen, then, if you have ears!

[16] "Now, to what can I compare the people of this day? They are like children sitting in the market place. One group shouts to the other, [17] 'We played wedding music for you, but you wouldn't dance! We sang funeral songs, but you wouldn't cry!' [18] When John came, he fasted and drank no wine, and everyone said, 'He has a demon in him!' [19] When the Son of Man came, he ate and drank, and everyone said, 'Look at this man! He is a glutton and a drinker, a friend of tax collectors and other outcasts!' God's wisdom, however, is shown to be true by its results."

The Unbelieving Towns
(Lk 10.13–15)

[20] The people in the towns where Jesus had performed most of his miracles did not turn from their sins, so he reproached those towns. [21] "How terrible it will be for you, Chorazin! How terrible for you too, Bethsaida! If the miracles which were performed in you had been performed

a **11.12** has suffered violent attacks; *or* has been coming violently.

in Tyre and Sidon, the people there would long ago have put on sackcloth and sprinkled ashes on themselves, to show that they had turned from their sins! ²² I assure you that on the Judgement Day God will show more mercy to the people of Tyre and Sidon than to you! ²³ And as for you, Capernaum! Did you want to lift yourself up to heaven? You will be thrown down to hell! If the miracles which were performed in you had been performed in Sodom, it would still be in existence today! ²⁴ You can be sure that on the Judgement Day God will show more mercy to Sodom than to you!"

Come to Me and Rest
(Lk 10.21–22)

²⁵ At that time Jesus said, "Father, Lord of heaven and earth! I thank you because you have shown to the unlearned what you have hidden from the wise and learned. ²⁶ Yes, Father, this was how you wanted it to happen.

²⁷ "My Father has given me all things. No one knows the Son except the Father, and no one knows the Father except the Son and those to whom the Son chooses to reveal him.

²⁸ "Come to me, all of you who are tired from carrying heavy loads, and I will give you rest. ²⁹ Take my yoke and put it on you, and learn from me, because I am gentle and humble in spirit; and you will find rest. ³⁰ For the yoke I will give you is easy, and the load I will put on you is light."

Come to me, all of you who are tired ...   (11.28)

The Question about the Sabbath
(Mk 2.23–28; Lk 6.1–5)

12 Not long afterwards Jesus was walking through some cornfields on the Sabbath. His disciples were hungry, so they began to pick ears of corn and eat the grain. ²When the Pharisees saw this, they said to Jesus, "Look, it is against our Law for your disciples to do this on the Sabbath!"

³Jesus answered, "Have you never read what David did that time when he and his men were hungry? ⁴He went into the house of God, and he and his men ate the bread offered to God, even though it was against the Law for them to eat it — only the priests were allowed to eat that bread. ⁵Or have you not read in the Law of Moses that every Sabbath the priests in the Temple actually break the Sabbath law, yet they are not guilty? ⁶I tell you that there is something here greater than the Temple. ⁷The scripture says, 'It is kindness that I want, not animal sacrifices.' If you really knew what this means, you would not condemn people who are not guilty; ⁸for the Son of Man is Lord of the Sabbath."

The Man with a Paralysed Hand
(Mk 3.1–6; Lk 6.6–11)

⁹Jesus left that place and went to a synagogue, ¹⁰where there was a man who had a paralysed hand. Some people were there who wanted to accuse Jesus of doing wrong, so they asked him, "Is it against our Law to heal on the Sabbath?"

¹¹Jesus answered, "What if one of you has a sheep and it falls into a deep hole on the Sabbath? Will you not take hold of it and lift it out? ¹²And a human being is worth much more than a sheep! So then, our Law does allow us to help someone on the Sabbath." ¹³Then he said to the man with the paralysed hand, "Stretch out your hand."

He stretched it out, and it became well again, just like the other one. ¹⁴Then the Pharisees left and made plans to kill Jesus.

God's Chosen Servant

¹⁵When Jesus heard about the plot against him, he went away from that place; and large crowds followed him. He

healed all those who were ill [16] and gave them orders not to tell others about him. [17] He did this so as to make what God had said through the prophet Isaiah come true:

[18] "Here is my servant, whom I have chosen,
　　　the one I love, and with whom I am pleased.
　I will send my Spirit upon him,
　　　and he will announce my judgement to the nations.
[19] He will not argue or shout,
　　　or make loud speeches in the streets.
[20] He will not break off a bent reed,
　　　or put out a flickering lamp.
　He will persist until he causes justice to triumph,
[21]　　and in him all peoples will put their hope."

Jesus and Beelzebul
(Mk 3.20–30; Lk 11.14–23)

[22] Then some people brought to Jesus a man who was blind and could not talk because he had a demon. Jesus healed the man, so that he was able to talk and see. [23] The crowds were all amazed at what Jesus had done. "Could he be the Son of David?" they asked.

[24] When the Pharisees heard this, they replied, "He drives out demons only because their ruler Beelzebul gives him power to do so."

[25] Jesus knew what they were thinking, so he said to them, "Any country that divides itself into groups which fight each other will not last very long. And any town or family that divides itself into groups which fight each other will fall apart. [26] So if one group is fighting another in Satan's kingdom, this means that it is already divided into groups and will soon fall apart! [27] You say that I drive out demons because Beelzebul gives me the power to do so. Well, then, who gives your followers the power to drive them out? What your own followers do proves that you are wrong! [28] No, it is not Beelzebul, but God's Spirit, who gives me the power to drive out demons, which proves that the Kingdom of God has already come upon you.

[29] "No one can break into a strong man's house and take away his belongings unless he first ties up the strong man; then he can plunder his house.

³⁰ "Anyone who is not for me is really against me; anyone who does not help me gather is really scattering. ³¹ And so I tell you that people can be forgiven any sin and any evil thing they say; [a] but whoever says evil things against the Holy Spirit will not be forgiven. ³² Anyone who says something against the Son of Man can be forgiven; but whoever says something against the Holy Spirit will not be forgiven — now or ever.

A Tree and its Fruit
(Lk 6.43–45)

³³ "To have good fruit you must have a healthy tree; if you have a poor tree, you will have bad fruit. A tree is known by the kind of fruit it bears. ³⁴ You snakes — how can you say good things when you are evil? For the mouth speaks what the heart is full of. ³⁵ A good person brings good things out of a treasure of good things; a bad person brings bad things out of a treasure of bad things.

³⁶ "You can be sure that on Judgement Day everyone will have to give account of every useless word he has ever spoken. ³⁷ Your words will be used to judge you — to declare you either innocent or guilty."

The Demand for a Miracle
(Mk 8.11–12; Lk 11.29–32)

³⁸ Then some teachers of the Law and some Pharisees spoke up. "Teacher," they said, "we want to see you perform a miracle."

³⁹ "How evil and godless are the people of this day!" Jesus exclaimed. "You ask me for a miracle? No! The only miracle you will be given is the miracle of the prophet Jonah. ⁴⁰ In the same way that Jonah spent three days and nights in the big fish, so will the Son of Man spend three days and nights in the depths of the earth. ⁴¹ On Judgement Day the people of Nineveh will stand up and accuse you, because they turned from their sins when they heard Jonah preach; and I tell you that there is something here greater than Jonah! ⁴² On Judgement Day the Queen of Sheba will stand up and accuse you, because she travelled all the way from her

a **12.31** evil thing they say; *or* evil thing they say against God.

country to listen to King Solomon's wise teaching; and I assure you that there is something here greater than Solomon!

The Return of the Evil Spirit
(Lk 11.24–26)

⁴³ "When an evil spirit goes out of a person, it travels over dry country looking for a place to rest. If it can't find one, ⁴⁴ it says to itself, 'I will go back to my house.' So it goes back and finds the house empty, clean, and all tidy. ⁴⁵ Then it goes out and brings along seven other spirits even worse than itself, and they come and live there. So when it is all over, that person is in a worse state than he was at the beginning. This is what will happen to the evil people of this day."

Jesus' Mother and Brothers
(Mk 3.31–35; Lk 8.19–21)

⁴⁶ Jesus was still talking to the people when his mother and brothers arrived. They stood outside, asking to speak with him. ⁴⁷ So one of the people there said to him, "Look, your mother and brothers are standing outside, and they want to speak with you." ª

⁴⁸ Jesus answered, "Who is my mother? Who are my brothers?" ⁴⁹ Then he pointed to his disciples and said, "Look! Here are my mother and my brothers! ⁵⁰ Whoever does what my Father in heaven wants him to do is my brother, my sister, and my mother."

The Parable of the Sower
(Mk 4.1–9; Lk 8.4–8)

13 That same day Jesus left the house and went to the lakeside, where he sat down to teach. ² The crowd that gathered round him was so large that he got into a boat and sat in it, while the crowd stood on the shore. ³ He used parables to tell them many things.

"Once there was a man who went out to sow corn. ⁴ As he scattered the seed in the field, some of it fell along the path, and the birds came and ate it up. ⁵ Some of it fell on rocky ground, where there was little soil. The seeds soon sprouted,

a **12.47** *Some manuscripts do not have verse 47.*

because the soil wasn't deep. ⁶But when the sun came up, it burnt the young plants; and because the roots had not grown deep enough, the plants soon dried up. ⁷Some of the seed fell among thorn bushes, which grew up and choked the plants. ⁸But some seeds fell in good soil, and the plants produced corn; some produced a hundred grains, others sixty, and others thirty."

⁹And Jesus concluded, "Listen, then, if you have ears!"

The Purpose of the Parables
(Mk 4.10–12; Lk 8.9–10)

¹⁰Then the disciples came to Jesus and asked him, "Why do you use parables when you talk to the people?"

¹¹Jesus answered, "The knowledge about the secrets of the Kingdom of heaven has been given to you, but not to them. ¹²For the person who has something will be given more, so that he will have more than enough; but the person who has nothing will have taken away from him even the little he has. ¹³The reason I use parables in talking to them is that they look, but do not see, and they listen, but do not hear or understand. ¹⁴So the prophecy of Isaiah applies to them:

'This people will listen and listen, but not understand;
    they will look and look, but not see,
¹⁵because their minds are dull,
    and they have stopped up their ears
    and have closed their eyes.
Otherwise, their eyes would see,
    their ears would hear,
    their minds would understand,
and they would turn to me, says God,
    and I would heal them.'

¹⁶"As for you, how fortunate you are! Your eyes see and your ears hear. ¹⁷I assure you that many prophets and many of God's people wanted very much to see what you see, but they could not, and to hear what you hear, but they did not.

Jesus Explains the Parable of the Sower
(Mk 4.13–20; Lk 8.11–15)

¹⁸"Listen, then, and learn what the parable of the sower means. ¹⁹Those who hear the message about the Kingdom

but do not understand it are like the seeds that fell along the path. The Evil One comes and snatches away what was sown in them. ²⁰The seeds that fell on rocky ground stand for those who receive the message gladly as soon as they hear it. ²¹But it does not sink deep into them, and they don't last long. So when trouble or persecution comes because of the message, they give up at once. ²²The seeds that fell among thorn bushes stand for those who hear the message; but the worries about this life and the love for riches choke the message, and they don't bear fruit. ²³And the seeds sown in the good soil stand for those who hear the message and understand it: they bear fruit, some as much as a hundred, others sixty, and others thirty."

The Parable of the Weeds

²⁴Jesus told them another parable: "The Kingdom of heaven is like this. A man sowed good seed in his field. ²⁵One night, when everyone was asleep, an enemy came and sowed weeds among the wheat and went away. ²⁶When the plants grew and the ears of corn began to form, then the weeds showed up. ²⁷The man's servants came to him and said, 'Sir, it was good seed you sowed in your field; where did the weeds come from?' ²⁸'It was some enemy who did this,' he answered. 'Do you want us to go and pull up the weeds?' they asked him. ²⁹'No,' he answered, 'because as you gather the weeds you might pull up some of the wheat along with them. ³⁰Let the wheat and the weeds both grow together until harvest. Then I will tell the harvest workers to pull up the weeds first, tie them in bundles and burn them, and then to gather in the wheat and put it in my barn.' "

The Parable of the Mustard Seed
(Mk 4.30–32; Lk 13.18–19)

³¹Jesus told them another parable: "The Kingdom of heaven is like this. A man takes a mustard seed and sows it in his field. ³²It is the smallest of all seeds, but when it grows up, it is the biggest of all plants. It becomes a tree, so that birds come and make their nests in its branches."

The Parable of the Yeast
(Lk 13.20–21)

33 Jesus told them still another parable: "The Kingdom of heaven is like this. A woman takes some yeast and mixes it with forty litres of flour until the whole batch of dough rises."

Jesus' Use of Parables
(Mk 4.33–34)

34 Jesus used parables to tell all these things to the crowds; he would not say a thing to them without using a parable. 35 He did this to make what the prophet had said come true:

"I will use parables when I speak to them;
   I will tell them things unknown since the creation of
   the world."

Jesus Explains the Parable of the Weeds

36 When Jesus had left the crowd and gone indoors, his disciples came to him and said, "Tell us what the parable about the weeds in the field means."

37 Jesus answered, "The man who sowed the good seed is the Son of Man; 38 the field is the world; the good seed is the people who belong to the Kingdom; the weeds are the people who belong to the Evil One; 39 and the enemy who sowed the weeds is the Devil. The harvest is the end of the age, and the harvest workers are angels. 40 Just as the weeds are gathered up and burnt in the fire, so the same thing will happen at the end of the age: 41 the Son of Man will send out his angels to gather up out of his Kingdom all those who cause people to sin and all others who do evil things, 42 and they will throw them into the fiery furnace, where they will cry and grind their teeth. 43 Then God's people will shine like the sun in their Father's Kingdom. Listen, then, if you have ears!

The Parable of the Hidden Treasure

44 "The Kingdom of heaven is like this. A man happens to find a treasure hidden in a field. He covers it up again, and is so happy that he goes and sells everything he has, and then goes back and buys that field.

The Parable of the Pearl

[45] "Also, the Kingdom of heaven is like this. A man is looking for fine pearls, [46] and when he finds one that is unusually fine, he goes and sells everything he has, and buys that pearl.

The Parable of the Net

[47] "Also, the Kingdom of heaven is like this. Some fishermen throw their net out in the lake and catch all kinds of fish. [48] When the net is full, they pull it to shore and sit down to divide the fish: the good ones go into their buckets, the worthless ones are thrown away. [49] It will be like this at the end of the age: the angels will go out and gather up the evil people from among the good [50] and will throw them into the fiery furnace, where they will cry and grind their teeth.

New Truths and Old

[51] "Do you understand these things?" Jesus asked them.

"Yes," they answered.

[52] So he replied, "This means, then, that every teacher of the Law who becomes a disciple in the Kingdom of heaven is like the owner of a house who takes new and old things out of his storeroom."

Jesus is Rejected at Nazareth
(Mk 6.1–6; Lk 4.16–30)

[53] When Jesus finished telling these parables, he left that place [54] and went back to his home town. He taught in the synagogue, and those who heard him were amazed. "Where did he get such wisdom?" they asked. "And what about his miracles? [55] Isn't he the carpenter's son? Isn't Mary his mother, and aren't James, Joseph, Simon, and Judas his brothers? [56] Aren't all his sisters living here? Where did he get all this?" [57] And so they rejected him.

Jesus said to them, "A prophet is respected everywhere except in his home town and by his own family." [58] Because they did not have faith, he did not perform many miracles there.

The Death of John the Baptist
(Mk 6.14–29; Lk 9.7–9)

14 At that time Herod, the ruler of Galilee, heard about Jesus. ²"He is really John the Baptist, who has come back to life," he told his officials. "That is why he has this power to perform miracles."

³For Herod had earlier ordered John's arrest, and he had him chained and put in prison. He had done this because of Herodias, his brother Philip's wife. ⁴For some time John the Baptist had told Herod, "It isn't right for you to be married to Herodias!" ⁵Herod wanted to kill him, but he was afraid of the Jewish people, because they considered John to be a prophet.

⁶On Herod's birthday the daughter of Herodias danced in front of the whole group. Herod was so pleased ⁷that he promised her, "I swear that I will give you anything you ask for!"

⁸At her mother's suggestion she asked him, "Give me here and now the head of John the Baptist on a dish!"

⁹The king was sad, but because of the promise he had made in front of all his guests he gave orders that her wish be granted. ¹⁰So he had John beheaded in prison. ¹¹The head was brought in on a dish and given to the girl, who took it to her mother. ¹²John's disciples came, carried away his body, and buried it; then they went and told Jesus.

Jesus Feeds a Great Crowd
(Mk 6.30–44; Lk 9.10–17; Jn 6.1–14)

¹³When Jesus heard the news about John, he left there in a boat and went to a lonely place by himself. The people heard about it, so they left their towns and followed him by land. ¹⁴Jesus got out of the boat, and when he saw the large crowd, his heart was filled with pity for them, and he healed those who were ill.

¹⁵That evening his disciples came to him and said, "It is already very late, and this is a lonely place. Send the people away and let them go to the villages to buy food for themselves."

¹⁶"They don't have to leave," answered Jesus. "You yourselves give them something to eat!"

¹⁷"All we have here are five loaves and two fish," they replied.

¹⁸ "Then bring them here to me," Jesus said. ¹⁹ He ordered the people to sit down on the grass; then he took the five loaves and the two fish, looked up to heaven, and gave thanks to God. He broke the loaves and gave them to the disciples, and the disciples gave them to the people. ²⁰ Everyone ate and had enough. Then the disciples took up twelve baskets full of what was left over. ²¹ The number of men who ate was about 5,000, not counting the women and children.

Jesus Walks on the Water
(Mk 6.45–52; Jn 6.15–21)

²² Then Jesus made the disciples get into the boat and go on ahead to the other side of the lake, while he sent the people away. ²³ After sending the people away, he went up a hill by himself to pray. When evening came, Jesus was there alone; ²⁴ and by this time the boat was far out in the lake, tossed about by the waves, because the wind was blowing against it.

²⁵ Between three and six o'clock in the morning Jesus came to the disciples, walking on the water. ²⁶ When they saw him walking on the water, they were terrified. "It's a ghost!" they said, and screamed with fear.

²⁷ Jesus spoke to them at once. "Courage!" he said. "It is I. Don't be afraid!"

²⁸ Then Peter spoke up. "Lord, if it is really you, order me to come out on the water to you."

²⁹ "Come!" answered Jesus. So Peter got out of the boat and started walking on the water to Jesus. ³⁰ But when he noticed the strong wind, he was afraid and started to sink down in the water. "Save me, Lord!" he cried.

³¹ At once Jesus reached out and grabbed hold of him and said, "How little faith you have! Why did you doubt?"

³² They both got into the boat, and the wind died down. ³³ Then the disciples in the boat worshipped Jesus. "Truly you are the Son of God!" they exclaimed.

Jesus Heals the Sick in Gennesaret
(Mk 6.53–56)

³⁴ They crossed the lake and came to land at Gennesaret, ³⁵ where the people recognized Jesus. So they sent for the sick people in all the surrounding country and brought them to

Jesus. ³⁶They begged him to let those who were ill at least touch the edge of his cloak; and all who touched it were made well.

The Teaching of the Ancestors
(Mk 7.1–13)

15 Then some Pharisees and teachers of the Law came from Jerusalem to Jesus and asked him, ²"Why is it that your disciples disobey the teaching handed down by our ancestors? They don't wash their hands in the proper way before they eat!"

³Jesus answered, "And why do you disobey God's command and follow your own teaching? ⁴For God said, 'Respect your father and your mother,' and 'Whoever curses his father or his mother is to be put to death.' ⁵But you teach that if a person has something he could use to help his father or mother, but says, 'This belongs to God,' ⁶he does not need to honour his father.ᵃ In this way you disregard God's command, in order to follow your own teaching. ⁷You hypocrites! How right Isaiah was when he prophesied about you!

⁸ 'These people, says God, honour me with their words,
     but their heart is really far away from me.

⁹ It is no use for them to worship me,
     because they teach human rules as though they were
       my laws!' "

The Things that Make a Person Unclean
(Mk 7.14–23)

¹⁰Then Jesus called the crowd to him and said to them, "Listen and understand! ¹¹It is not what goes into a person's mouth that makes him ritually unclean; rather, what comes out of it makes him unclean."

¹²Then the disciples came to him and said, "Do you know that the Pharisees had their feelings hurt by what you said?"

¹³"Every plant which my Father in heaven did not plant will be pulled up," answered Jesus. ¹⁴"Don't worry about them! They are blind leaders of the blind; and when one blind man leads another, both fall into a ditch."

¹⁵Peter spoke up, "Explain this saying to us."

a **15.6** his father; *some manuscripts have* his father or mother.

Things that come out of the mouth come from the heart ... (15.18)

¹⁶ Jesus said to them, "You are still no more intelligent than the others. ¹⁷ Don't you understand? Anything that goes into a person's mouth goes into his stomach and then on out of his body. ¹⁸ But the things that come out of the mouth come from the heart, and these are the things that make a person ritually unclean. ¹⁹ For from his heart come the evil ideas which lead him to kill, commit adultery, and do other immoral things; to rob, lie, and slander others. ²⁰ These are the things that make a person unclean. But to eat without washing your hands as they say you should — this doesn't make a person unclean."

A Woman's Faith
(Mk 7.24–30)

²¹ Jesus left that place and went off to the territory near the cities of Tyre and Sidon. ²² A Canaanite woman who lived in that region came to him. "Son of David!" she cried out. "Have mercy on me, sir! My daughter has a demon and is in a terrible condition."

²³ But Jesus did not say a word to her. His disciples came to him and begged him, "Send her away! She is following us and making all this noise!"

²⁴ Then Jesus replied, "I have been sent only to the lost sheep of the people of Israel."

²⁵At this the woman came and fell at his feet. "Help me, sir!" she said.

²⁶Jesus answered, "It isn't right to take the children's food and throw it to the dogs."

²⁷"That's true, sir," she answered; "but even the dogs eat the leftovers that fall from their masters' table."

²⁸So Jesus answered her, "You are a woman of great faith! What you want will be done for you." And at that very moment her daughter was healed.

Jesus Heals Many People

²⁹Jesus left there and went along by Lake Galilee. He climbed a hill and sat down. ³⁰Large crowds came to him, bringing with them the lame, the blind, the crippled, the dumb, and many other sick people, whom they placed at Jesus' feet; and he healed them. ³¹The people were amazed as they saw the dumb speaking, the crippled made whole, the lame walking, and the blind seeing; and they praised the God of Israel.

Jesus Feeds Another Great Crowd
(Mk 8.1–10)

³²Jesus called his disciples to him and said, "I feel sorry for these people, because they have been with me for three days and now have nothing to eat. I don't want to send them away without feeding them, for they might faint on their way home."

³³The disciples asked him, "Where will we find enough food in this desert to feed this crowd?"

³⁴"How much bread have you?" Jesus asked.

"Seven loaves," they answered, "and a few small fish."

³⁵So Jesus ordered the crowd to sit down on the ground. ³⁶Then he took the seven loaves and the fish, gave thanks to God, broke them, and gave them to the disciples; and the disciples gave them to the people. ³⁷They all ate and had enough. Then the disciples took up seven baskets full of pieces left over. ³⁸The number of men who ate was 4,000, not counting the women and children.

³⁹Then Jesus sent the people away, got into a boat, and went to the territory of Magadan.

The Demand for a Miracle
(Mk 8.11–13; Lk 12.54–56)

16 Some Pharisees and Sadducees who came to Jesus wanted to trap him, so they asked him to perform a miracle for them, to show that God approved of him. ²But Jesus answered, "When the sun is setting, you say, 'We are going to have fine weather, because the sky is red.' ³And early in the morning you say, 'It is going to rain, because the sky is red and dark.' You can predict the weather by looking at the sky, but you cannot interpret the signs concerning these times!ᵃ ⁴How evil and godless are the people of this day! You ask me for a miracle? No! The only miracle you will be given is the miracle of Jonah."

So he left them and went away.

The Yeast of the Pharisees and Sadducees
(Mk 8.14–21)

⁵When the disciples crossed over to the other side of the lake, they forgot to take any bread. ⁶Jesus said to them, "Take care; be on your guard against the yeast of the Pharisees and Sadducees."

⁷They started discussing among themselves, "He says this because we didn't bring any bread."

⁸Jesus knew what they were saying, so he asked them, "Why are you discussing among yourselves about not having any bread? How little faith you have! ⁹Don't you understand yet? Don't you remember when I broke the five loaves for the five thousand men? How many baskets did you fill? ¹⁰And what about the seven loaves for the four thousand men? How many baskets did you fill? ¹¹How is it that you don't understand that I was not talking to you about bread? Guard yourselves from the yeast of the Pharisees and Sadducees!"

¹²Then the disciples understood that he was not warning them to guard themselves from the yeast used in bread but from the teaching of the Pharisees and Sadducees.

a **16.3** *Some manuscripts do not have the words of Jesus in verses 2–3.*

Peter's Declaration about Jesus
(Mk 8.27–30; Lk 9.18–21)

[13] Jesus went to the territory near the town of Caesarea Philippi, where he asked his disciples, "Who do people say the Son of Man is?"

[14] "Some say John the Baptist," they answered. "Others say Elijah, while others say Jeremiah or some other prophet."

[15] "What about you?" he asked them. "Who do you say I am?"

[16] Simon Peter answered, "You are the Messiah, the Son of the living God."

[17] "Good for you, Simon son of John!" answered Jesus. "For this truth did not come to you from any human being, but it was given to you directly by my Father in heaven. [18] And so I tell you, Peter: you are a rock, and on this rock foundation I will build my church, and not even death will ever be able to overcome it. [19] I will give you the keys of the Kingdom of heaven; what you prohibit on earth will be prohibited in heaven, and what you permit on earth will be permitted in heaven."

[20] Then Jesus ordered his disciples not to tell anyone that he was the Messiah.

Jesus Speaks about his Suffering and Death
(Mk 8.31—9.1; Lk 9.22–27)

[21] From that time on Jesus began to say plainly to his disciples, "I must go to Jerusalem and suffer much from the elders, the chief priests, and the teachers of the Law. I will be put to death, but three days later I will be raised to life."

[22] Peter took him aside and began to rebuke him. "God forbid it, Lord!" he said. "That must never happen to you!"

[23] Jesus turned around and said to Peter, "Get away from me, Satan! You are an obstacle in my way, because these thoughts of yours don't come from God, but from human nature."

[24] Then Jesus said to his disciples, "If anyone wants to come with me, he must forget self, carry his cross, and follow me. [25] For whoever wants to save his own life will lose it; but whoever loses his life for my sake will find it. [26] Will people gain anything if they win the whole world but lose their life?

Of course not! There is nothing they can give to regain their life. ²⁷ For the Son of Man is about to come in the glory of his Father with his angels, and then he will reward each one according to his deeds. ²⁸ I assure you that there are some here who will not die until they have seen the Son of Man come as King."

The Transfiguration
(Mk 9.2–13; Lk 9.28–36)

17 Six days later Jesus took with him Peter and the brothers James and John and led them up a high mountain where they were alone. ² As they looked on, a change came over Jesus: his face was shining like the sun, and his clothes were dazzling white. ³ Then the three disciples saw Moses and Elijah talking with Jesus. ⁴ So Peter spoke up and said to Jesus, "Lord, how good it is that we are here! If you wish, I will make three tents here, one for you, one for Moses, and one for Elijah."

⁵ While he was talking, a shining cloud came over them, and a voice from the cloud said, "This is my own dear Son, with whom I am pleased — listen to him!"

⁶ When the disciples heard the voice, they were so terrified that they threw themselves face downwards on the ground. ⁷ Jesus came to them and touched them. "Get up," he said. "Don't be afraid!" ⁸ So they looked up and saw no one there but Jesus.

⁹ As they came down the mountain, Jesus ordered them, "Don't tell anyone about this vision you have seen until the Son of Man has been raised from death."

¹⁰ Then the disciples asked Jesus, "Why do the teachers of the Law say that Elijah has to come first?"

¹¹ "Elijah is indeed coming first," answered Jesus, "and he will get everything ready. ¹² But I tell you that Elijah has already come and people did not recognize him, but treated him just as they pleased. In the same way they will also ill-treat the Son of Man."

¹³ Then the disciples understood that he was talking to them about John the Baptist.

Jesus Heals a Boy with a Demon
(Mk 9.14–29; Lk 9.37–43a)

[14]When they returned to the crowd, a man came to Jesus, knelt before him, [15]and said, "Sir, have mercy on my son! He is an epileptic and has such terrible fits that he often falls in the fire or into water. [16]I brought him to your disciples, but they could not heal him."

[17]Jesus answered, "How unbelieving and wrong you people are! How long must I stay with you? How long do I have to put up with you? Bring the boy here to me!" [18]Jesus gave a command to the demon, and it went out of the boy, and at that very moment he was healed.

[19]Then the disciples came to Jesus in private and asked him, "Why couldn't we drive the demon out?"

[20]"It was because you haven't enough faith," answered Jesus. "I assure you that if you have faith as big as a mustard seed, you can say to this hill, 'Go from here to there!' and it will go. You could do anything!"[a]

Jesus Speaks Again about his Death
(Mk 9.30–32; Lk 9.43b–45)

[22]When the disciples all came together in Galilee, Jesus said to them, "The Son of Man is about to be handed over to people [23]who will kill him; but three days later he will be raised to life."

The disciples became very sad.

Payment of the Temple Tax

[24]When Jesus and his disciples came to Capernaum, the collectors of the temple tax came to Peter and asked, "Does your teacher pay the temple tax?"

[25]"Of course," Peter answered.

When Peter went into the house, Jesus spoke up first, "Simon, what is your opinion? Who pays duties or taxes to the kings of this world? The citizens of the country or the foreigners?"

[26]"The foreigners," answered Peter.

a **17.20** *Some manuscripts add verse 21:* But only prayer and fasting can drive this kind out; nothing else can *(see Mk 9.29).*

"Well, then," replied Jesus, "that means that the citizens don't have to pay. ²⁷But we don't want to offend these people. So go to the lake and drop in a line. Pull up the first fish you hook, and in its mouth you will find a coin worth enough for my temple tax and yours. Take it and pay them our taxes."

Who is the Greatest?
(Mk 9.33–37; Lk 9.46–48)

18 At that time the disciples came to Jesus, asking, "Who is the greatest in the Kingdom of heaven?"

²So Jesus called a child, made him stand in front of them, ³and said, "I assure you that unless you change and become like children, you will never enter the Kingdom of heaven. ⁴The greatest in the Kingdom of heaven is the one who humbles himself and becomes like this child. ⁵And whoever welcomes in my name one such child as this, welcomes me.

... one such child as this, welcomes me. (18.5)

Temptations to Sin
(Mk 9.42–48; Lk 17.1–2)

⁶"If anyone should cause one of these little ones to lose his faith in me, it would be better for that person to have a large millstone tied round his neck and be drowned in the deep sea. ⁷How terrible for the world that there are things that make people lose their faith! Such things will always happen — but how terrible for the one who causes them!

⁸"If your hand or your foot makes you lose your faith, cut it off and throw it away! It is better for you to enter life without a hand or a foot than to keep both hands and both feet and be thrown into the eternal fire. ⁹And if your eye makes you

lose your faith, take it out and throw it away! It is better for you to enter life with only one eye than to keep both eyes and be thrown into the fire of hell.

The Parable of the Lost Sheep
(Lk 15.3–7)

10 "See that you don't despise any of these little ones. Their angels in heaven, I tell you, are always in the presence of my Father in heaven. [a]

12 "What do you think a man does who has a hundred sheep and one of them gets lost? He will leave the other ninety-nine grazing on the hillside and go and look for the lost sheep. 13 When he finds it, I tell you, he feels far happier over this one sheep than over the ninety-nine that did not get lost. 14 In just the same way your [b] Father in heaven does not want any of these little ones to be lost.

He will ... go and look for the lost sheep   (18.12)

A Brother or Sister who Sins

15 "If your brother sins against you, [c] go to him and show him his fault. But do it privately, just between yourselves.

a **18.10** *Some manuscripts add verse 11:* For the Son of Man came to save the lost *(see Lk 19.10).*
b **18.14** your; *some manuscripts have* my.
c **18.15** *Some manuscripts do not have* against you.

If he listens to you, you have won your brother back. ¹⁶ But if he will not listen to you, take one or two other persons with you, so that 'every accusation may be upheld by the testimony of two or more witnesses,' as the scripture says. ¹⁷ And if he will not listen to them, then tell the whole thing to the church. Finally, if he will not listen to the church, treat him as though he were a pagan or a tax collector.

Prohibiting and Permitting

¹⁸ "And so I tell all of you: what you prohibit on earth will be prohibited in heaven, and what you permit on earth will be permitted in heaven.

¹⁹ "And I tell you more: whenever two of you on earth agree about anything you pray for, it will be done for you by my Father in heaven. ²⁰ For where two or three come together in my name, I am there with them."

The Parable of the Unforgiving Servant

²¹ Then Peter came to Jesus and asked, "Lord, if my brother keeps on sinning against me, how many times do I have to forgive him? Seven times?"

²² "No, not seven times," answered Jesus, "but seventy times seven, ª ²³ because the Kingdom of heaven is like this. Once there was a king who decided to check on his servants' accounts. ²⁴ He had just begun to do so when one of them was brought in who owed him millions of pounds. ²⁵ The servant did not have enough to pay his debt, so the king ordered him to be sold as a slave, with his wife and his children and all that he had, in order to pay the debt. ²⁶ The servant fell on his knees before the king. 'Be patient with me,' he begged, 'and I will pay you everything!' ²⁷ The king felt sorry for him, so he forgave him the debt and let him go.

²⁸ "Then the man went out and met one of his fellow-servants who owed him a few pounds. He grabbed him and started choking him. 'Pay back what you owe me!' he said. ²⁹ His fellow-servant fell down and begged him, 'Be patient with me, and I will pay you back!' ³⁰ But he refused; instead, he had him

a 18.22 seventy times seven; *or* seventy-seven times.

thrown into jail until he should pay the debt. [31] When the other servants saw what had happened, they were very upset and went to the king and told him everything. [32] So he called the servant in. 'You worthless slave!' he said. 'I forgave you the whole amount you owed me, just because you asked me to. [33] You should have had mercy on your fellow-servant, just as I had mercy on you.' [34] The king was very angry, and he sent the servant to jail to be punished until he should pay back the whole amount."

[35] And Jesus concluded, "That is how my Father in heaven will treat every one of you unless you forgive your brother from your heart."

Jesus Teaches about Divorce
(Mk 10.1–12)

19 When Jesus finished saying these things, he left Galilee and went to the territory of Judea on the other side of the River Jordan. [2] Large crowds followed him, and he healed them there.

[3] Some Pharisees came to him and tried to trap him by asking, "Does our Law allow a man to divorce his wife for whatever reason he wishes?"

[4] Jesus answered, "Haven't you read the scripture that says that in the beginning the Creator made people male and female? [5] And God said, 'For this reason a man will leave his father and mother and unite with his wife, and the two will become one.' [6] So they are no longer two, but one. No human being must separate, then, what God has joined together."

[7] The Pharisees asked him, "Why, then, did Moses give the law for a man to hand his wife a divorce notice and send her away?"

[8] Jesus answered, "Moses gave you permission to divorce your wives because you are so hard to teach. But it was not like that at the time of creation. [9] I tell you, then, that any man who divorces his wife for any cause other than her unfaithfulness, commits adultery if he marries some other woman."

[10] His disciples said to him, "If this is how it is between a man and his wife, it is better not to marry."

[11] Jesus answered, "This teaching does not apply to everyone, but only to those to whom God has given it. [12] For there

are different reasons why men cannot marry: some, because they were born that way; others, because men made them that way; and others do not marry for the sake of the Kingdom of heaven. Let him who can accept this teaching do so."

Jesus Blesses Little Children
(Mk 10.13–16; Lk 18.15–17)

¹³ Some people brought children to Jesus for him to place his hands on them and to pray for them, but the disciples scolded the people. ¹⁴ Jesus said, "Let the children come to me and do not stop them, because the Kingdom of heaven belongs to such as these."

¹⁵ He placed his hands on them and then went away.

The Rich Young Man
(Mk 10.17–31; Lk 18.18–30)

¹⁶ Once a man came to Jesus. "Teacher," he asked, "what good thing must I do to receive eternal life?"

¹⁷ "Why do you ask me concerning what is good?" answered Jesus. "There is only One who is good. Keep the commandments if you want to enter life."

¹⁸ "What commandments?" he asked.

Jesus answered, "Do not commit murder; do not commit adultery; do not steal; do not accuse anyone falsely; ¹⁹ respect your father and your mother; and love your neighbour as you love yourself."

²⁰ "I have obeyed all these commandments," the young man replied. "What else do I need to do?"

²¹ Jesus said to him, "If you want to be perfect, go and sell all you have and give the money to the poor, and you will have riches in heaven; then come and follow me."

²² When the young man heard this, he went away sad, because he was very rich.

²³ Jesus then said to his disciples, "I assure you: it will be very hard for rich people to enter the Kingdom of heaven. ²⁴ I repeat: it is much harder for a rich person to enter the Kingdom of God than for a camel to go through the eye of a needle."

²⁵ When the disciples heard this, they were completely amazed. "Who, then, can be saved?" they asked.

²⁶Jesus looked straight at them and answered, "This is impossible for human beings, but for God everything is possible."

²⁷Then Peter spoke up. "Look," he said, "we have left everything and followed you. What will we have?"

²⁸Jesus said to them, "You can be sure that when the Son of Man sits on his glorious throne in the New Age, then you twelve followers of mine will also sit on thrones, to rule the twelve tribes of Israel. ²⁹And everyone who has left houses or brothers or sisters or father or mother or children or fields for my sake, will receive a hundred times more and will be given eternal life. ³⁰But many who now are first will be last, and many who now are last will be first.

The Workers in the Vineyard

20 "The Kingdom of heaven is like this. Once there was a man who went out early in the morning to hire some men to work in his vineyard. ²He agreed to pay them the regular wage, a silver coin a day, and sent them to work in his vineyard. ³He went out again to the market place at nine o'clock and saw some men standing there doing nothing, ⁴so he told them, 'You also go and work in the vineyard, and I will pay you a fair wage.' ⁵So they went. Then at twelve o'clock and again at three o'clock he did the same thing. ⁶It was nearly five o'clock when he went to the market place and saw some other men still standing there. 'Why are you wasting the whole day here doing nothing?' he asked them. ⁷'No one hired us,' they answered. 'Well, then, you also go and work in the vineyard,' he told them.

⁸"When evening came, the owner told his foreman, 'Call the workers and pay them their wages, starting with those who were hired last and ending with those who were hired first.' ⁹The men who had begun to work at five o'clock were paid a silver coin each. ¹⁰So when the men who were the first to be hired came to be paid, they thought they would get more; but they too were given a silver coin each. ¹¹They took their money and started grumbling against the employer. ¹²'These men who were hired last worked only one hour,' they said, 'while we put up with a whole day's work in the hot sun — yet you paid them the same as you paid us!'

¹³ " 'Listen, friend,' the owner answered one of them, 'I have not cheated you. After all, you agreed to do a day's work for one silver coin. ¹⁴ Now take your pay and go home. I want to give this man who was hired last as much as I have given you. ¹⁵ Don't I have the right to do as I wish with my own money? Or are you jealous because I am generous?' "

¹⁶ And Jesus concluded, "So those who are last will be first, and those who are first will be last."

Jesus Speaks a Third Time about his Death
(Mk 10.32–34; Lk 18.31–34)

¹⁷ As Jesus was going up to Jerusalem, he took the twelve disciples aside and spoke to them privately, as they walked along. ¹⁸ "Listen," he told them, "we are going up to Jerusalem, where the Son of Man will be handed over to the chief priests and the teachers of the Law. They will condemn him to death ¹⁹ and then hand him over to the Gentiles, who will mock him, whip him, and crucify him; but three days later he will be raised to life."

A Mother's Request
(Mk 10.35–45)

²⁰ Then the wife of Zebedee came to Jesus with her two sons, bowed before him, and asked him a favour.

²¹ "What do you want?" Jesus asked her.

She answered, "Promise me that these two sons of mine will sit at your right and your left when you are King."

²² "You don't know what you are asking for," Jesus answered the sons. "Can you drink the cup of suffering that I am about to drink?"

"We can," they answered.

²³ "You will indeed drink from my cup," Jesus told them, "but I do not have the right to choose who will sit at my right and my left. These places belong to those for whom my Father has prepared them."

²⁴ When the other ten disciples heard about this, they became angry with the two brothers. ²⁵ So Jesus called them all together and said, "You know that the rulers of the heathen have power over them, and the leaders have complete authority. ²⁶ This, however, is not the way it shall be among you.

If one of you wants to be great, he must be the servant of the rest; [27] and if one of you wants to be first, he must be your slave — [28] like the Son of Man, who did not come to be served, but to serve and to give his life to redeem many people."

Jesus Heals Two Blind Men
(Mk 10.46–52; Lk 18.35–43)

[29] As Jesus and his disciples were leaving Jericho, a large crowd was following. [30] Two blind men who were sitting by the road heard that Jesus was passing by, so they began to shout, "Son of David! Take pity on us, sir!"

[31] The crowd scolded them and told them to be quiet. But they shouted even more loudly, "Son of David! Take pity on us, sir!"

[32] Jesus stopped and called them. "What do you want me to do for you?" he asked them.

[33] "Sir," they answered, "we want you to give us our sight!"

[34] Jesus had pity on them and touched their eyes; at once they were able to see, and they followed him.

The Triumphant Entry into Jerusalem
(Mk 11.1–11; Lk 19.28–40; Jn 12.12–19)

21 As Jesus and his disciples approached Jerusalem, they came to Bethphage at the Mount of Olives. There Jesus sent two of the disciples on ahead [2] with these instructions: "Go to the village there ahead of you, and at once you will find a donkey tied up with her colt beside her. Untie them and bring them to me. [3] And if anyone says anything, tell him, 'The Master[a] needs them'; and then he will let them go at once."

[4] This happened in order to make what the prophet had said come true:

[5] "Tell the city of Zion,
    Look, your king is coming to you!
   He is humble and rides on a donkey
       and on a colt, the foal of a donkey."

a **21.3** The Master; *or* Their owner.

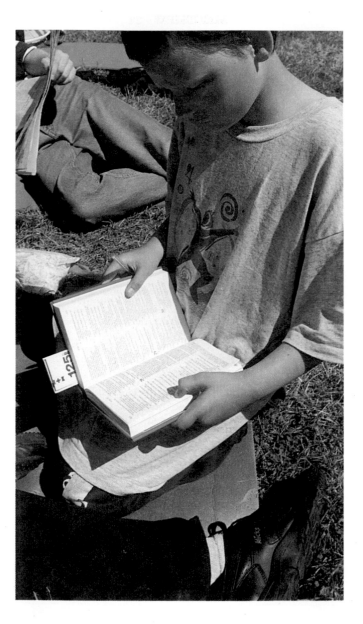

⁶So the disciples went and did what Jesus had told them to do: ⁷they brought the donkey and the colt, threw their cloaks over them, and Jesus got on. ⁸A large crowd of people spread their cloaks on the road while others cut branches from the trees and spread them on the road. ⁹The crowds walking in front of Jesus and those walking behind began to shout, "Praise to David's Son! God bless him who comes in the name of the Lord! Praise God!"

¹⁰When Jesus entered Jerusalem, the whole city was thrown into an uproar. "Who is he?" the people asked.

¹¹"This is the prophet Jesus, from Nazareth in Galilee," the crowds answered.

Jesus Goes to the Temple
(Mk 11.15–19; Lk 19.45–48; Jn 2.13–22)

¹²Jesus went into the Temple and drove out all those who were buying and selling there. He overturned the tables of the moneychangers and the stools of those who sold pigeons, ¹³and said to them, "It is written in the Scriptures that God said, 'My Temple will be called a house of prayer.' But you are making it a hideout for thieves!"

¹⁴The blind and the crippled came to him in the Temple, and he healed them. ¹⁵The chief priests and the teachers of the Law became angry when they saw the wonderful things he was doing and the children shouting in the Temple, "Praise to David's Son!" ¹⁶So they asked Jesus, "Do you hear what they are saying?"

"Indeed I do," answered Jesus. "Haven't you ever read this scripture? 'You have trained children and babies to offer perfect praise.' "

¹⁷Jesus left them and went out of the city to Bethany, where he spent the night.

Jesus Curses the Fig Tree
(Mk 11.12–14, 20–24)

¹⁸On his way back to the city early next morning, Jesus was hungry. ¹⁹He saw a fig tree by the side of the road and went to it, but found nothing on it except leaves. So he said to the tree, "You will never again bear fruit!" At once the fig tree dried up.

²⁰ The disciples saw this and were astounded. "How did the fig tree dry up so quickly?" they asked.

²¹ Jesus answered, "I assure you that if you believe and do not doubt, you will be able to do what I have done to this fig tree. And not only this, but you will even be able to say to this hill, 'Get up and throw yourself in the sea,' and it will. ²² If you believe, you will receive whatever you ask for in prayer."

The Question about Jesus' Authority
(Mk 11.27–33; Lk 20.1–8)

²³ Jesus came back to the Temple; and as he taught, the chief priests and the elders came to him and asked, "What right have you to do these things? Who gave you this right?"

²⁴ Jesus answered them, "I will ask you just one question, and if you give me an answer, I will tell you what right I have to do these things. ²⁵ Where did John's right to baptize come from: was it from God or from human beings?"

They started to argue among themselves, "What shall we say? If we answer, 'From God,' he will say to us, 'Why, then, did you not believe John?' ²⁶ But if we say, 'From human beings,' we are afraid of what the people might do, because they are all convinced that John was a prophet." ²⁷ So they answered Jesus, "We don't know."

And he said to them, "Neither will I tell you, then, by what right I do these things.

The Parable of the Two Sons

²⁸ "Now, what do you think? There was once a man who had two sons. He went to the elder one and said, 'Son, go and work in the vineyard today.' ²⁹ 'I don't want to,' he answered, but later he changed his mind and went. ³⁰ Then the father went to the other son and said the same thing. 'Yes, sir,' he answered, but he did not go. ³¹ Which one of the two did what his father wanted?"

"The elder one," they answered.

So Jesus said to them, "I tell you: the tax collectors and the prostitutes are going into the Kingdom of God ahead of you. ³² For John the Baptist came to you showing you the right path to take, and you would not believe him; but the tax collectors and the prostitutes believed him. Even when you saw this, you did not later change your minds and believe him.

The Parable of the Tenants in the Vineyard
(Mk 12.1–12; Lk 20.9–19)

[33] "Listen to another parable," Jesus said. "There was once a landowner who planted a vineyard, put a fence around it, dug a hole for the winepress, and built a watchtower. Then he let out the vineyard to tenants and went on a journey. [34] When the time came to gather the grapes, he sent his slaves to the tenants to receive his share of the harvest. [35] The tenants seized his slaves, beat one, killed another, and stoned another. [36] Again the man sent other slaves, more than the first time, and the tenants treated them the same way. [37] Last of all he sent his son to them. 'Surely they will respect my son,' he said. [38] But when the tenants saw the son, they said to themselves, 'This is the owner's son. Come on, let's kill him, and we will get his property!' [39] So they seized him, threw him out of the vineyard, and killed him.

[40] "Now, when the owner of the vineyard comes, what will he do to those tenants?" Jesus asked.

[41] "He will certainly kill those evil men," they answered, "and let the vineyard out to other tenants, who will give him his share of the harvest at the right time."

[42] Jesus said to them, "Haven't you ever read what the Scriptures say?

'The stone which the builders rejected as worthless
    turned out to be the most important of all.
This was done by the Lord;
    what a wonderful sight it is!'

[43] "And so I tell you," added Jesus, "the Kingdom of God will be taken away from you and given to a people who will produce the proper fruits." [a]

[45] The chief priests and the Pharisees heard Jesus' parables and knew that he was talking about them, [46] so they tried to arrest him. But they were afraid of the crowds, who considered Jesus to be a prophet.

a **21.43** *Some manuscripts add verse 44:* Whoever falls on this stone will be cut to pieces; and if the stone falls on someone, it will crush him to dust *(see Lk 20.18).*

The Parable of the Wedding Feast
(Lk 14.15–24)

22 Jesus again used parables in talking to the people. 2 "The Kingdom of heaven is like this. Once there was a king who prepared a wedding feast for his son. 3 He sent his servants to tell the invited guests to come to the feast, but they did not want to come. 4 So he sent other servants with this message for the guests: 'My feast is ready now; my bullocks and prize calves have been butchered, and everything is ready. Come to the wedding feast!' 5 But the invited guests paid no attention and went about their business: one went to his farm, another to his shop, 6 while others grabbed the servants, beat them, and killed them. 7 The king was very angry; so he sent his soldiers, who killed those murderers and burnt down their city. 8 Then he called his servants and said to them, 'My wedding feast is ready, but the people I invited did not deserve it. 9 Now go to the main streets and invite to the feast as many people as you find.' 10 So the servants went out into the streets and gathered all the people they could find, good and bad alike; and the wedding hall was filled with people.

11 "The king went in to look at the guests and saw a man who was not wearing wedding clothes. 12 'Friend, how did you get in here without wedding clothes?' the king asked him. But the man said nothing. 13 Then the king told the servants, 'Tie him up hand and foot, and throw him outside in the dark. There he will cry and grind his teeth.' "

14 And Jesus concluded, "Many are invited, but few are chosen."

The Question about Paying Taxes
(Mk 12.13–17; Lk 20.20–26)

15 The Pharisees went off and made a plan to trap Jesus with questions. 16 Then they sent to him some of their disciples and some members of Herod's party. "Teacher," they said, "we know that you tell the truth. You teach the truth about God's will for people, without worrying about what others think, because you pay no attention to anyone's status. 17 Tell us, then, what do you think? Is it against our Law to pay taxes to the Roman Emperor, or not?"

[18]Jesus, however, was aware of their evil plan, and so he said, "You hypocrites! Why are you trying to trap me? [19]Show me the coin for paying the tax!"

They brought him the coin, [20]and he asked them, "Whose face and name are these?"

[21]"The Emperor's," they answered.

So Jesus said to them, "Well, then, pay the Emperor what belongs to the Emperor, and pay God what belongs to God."

[22]When they heard this, they were amazed; and they left him and went away.

The Question about Rising from Death
(Mk 12.18–27; Lk 20.27–40)

[23]That same day some Sadducees came to Jesus and claimed that people will not rise from death. [24]"Teacher," they said, "Moses said that if a man who has no children dies, his brother must marry the widow so that they can have children who will be considered the dead man's children. [25]Now, there were seven brothers who used to live here. The eldest got married and died without having children, so he left his widow to his brother. [26]The same thing happened to the second brother, to the third, and finally to all seven. [27]Last of all, the woman died. [28]Now, on the day when the dead rise to life, whose wife will she be? All of them had married her."

[29]Jesus answered them, "How wrong you are! It is because you don't know the Scriptures or God's power. [30]For when the dead rise to life, they will be like the angels in heaven and will not marry. [31]Now, as for the dead rising to life: haven't you ever read what God has told you? He said, [32]'I am the God of Abraham, the God of Isaac, and the God of Jacob.' He is the God of the living, not of the dead."

[33]When the crowds heard this, they were amazed at his teaching.

The Great Commandment
(Mk 12.28–34; Lk 10.25–28)

[34]When the Pharisees heard that Jesus had silenced the Sadducees, they came together, [35]and one of them, a teacher of the Law, tried to trap him with a question. [36]"Teacher," he asked, "which is the greatest commandment in the Law?"

[37] Jesus answered, " 'Love the Lord your God with all your heart, with all your soul, and with all your mind.' [38] This is the greatest and the most important commandment. [39] The second most important commandment is like it: 'Love your neighbour as you love yourself.' [40] The whole Law of Moses and the teachings of the prophets depend on these two commandments."

The Question about the Messiah
(Mk 12.35–37; Lk 20.41–44)

[41] When some Pharisees gathered together, Jesus asked them, [42] "What do you think about the Messiah? Whose descendant is he?"

"He is David's descendant," they answered.

[43] "Why, then," Jesus asked, "did the Spirit inspire David to call him 'Lord'? David said,
[44] 'The Lord said to my Lord:
    Sit here on my right
    until I put your enemies under your feet.'
[45] If, then, David called him 'Lord', how can the Messiah be David's descendant?"

[46] No one was able to give Jesus any answer, and from that day on no one dared to ask him any more questions.

Jesus Warns against the Teachers of the Law and the Pharisees
(Mk 12.38–39; Lk 11.43, 46; 20.45–46)

23 Then Jesus spoke to the crowds and to his disciples. [2] "The teachers of the Law and the Pharisees are the authorized interpreters of Moses' Law. [3] So you must obey and follow everything they tell you to do; do not, however, imitate their actions, because they don't practise what they preach. [4] They tie on to people's backs loads that are heavy and hard to carry, yet they aren't willing even to lift a finger to help them carry those loads. [5] They do everything so that people will see them. Look at the straps with scripture verses on them which they wear on their foreheads and arms, and notice how large they are! Notice also how long are the tassels on their cloaks![a] [6] They love the best places at feasts and the

a **23.5** TASSELS ON THEIR CLOAKS: *These tassels were worn as a sign of devotion to God (see Num 15.37–41).*

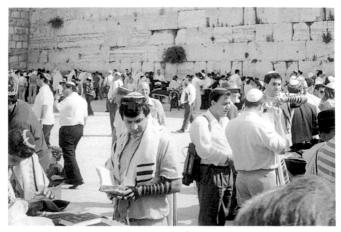

Look at the straps with Scripture verses ...   (23.5)

reserved seats in the synagogues; 7 they love to be greeted with respect in the market places and to be called 'Teacher'. 8 You must not be called 'Teacher', because you are all members of one family and have only one Teacher. 9 And you must not call anyone here on earth 'Father', because you have only the one Father in heaven. 10 Nor should you be called 'Leader', because your one and only leader is the Messiah. 11 The greatest one among you must be your servant. 12 Whoever makes himself great will be humbled, and whoever humbles himself will be made great.

Jesus Condemns their Hypocrisy
(Mk 12.40; Lk 11.39–42, 44, 52; 20.47)

13 "How terrible for you, teachers of the Law and Pharisees! You hypocrites! You lock the door to the Kingdom of heaven in people's faces, and you yourselves don't go in, nor do you allow in those who are trying to enter! a

a **23.13** *Some manuscripts add verse 14:* How terrible for you, teachers of the Law and Pharisees! You hypocrites! You take advantage of widows and rob them of their homes, and then make a show of saying long prayers! Because of this your punishment will be all the worse! *(see Mk 12.40).*

¹⁵ "How terrible for you, teachers of the Law and Pharisees! You hypocrites! You sail the seas and cross whole countries to win one convert; and when you succeed, you make him twice as deserving of going to hell as you yourselves are!

... but swallow a camel!   (23.24)

¹⁶ "How terrible for you, blind guides! You teach, 'If someone swears by the Temple, he isn't bound by his vow; but if he swears by the gold in the Temple, he is bound.' ¹⁷ Blind fools! Which is more important, the gold or the Temple which makes the gold holy? ¹⁸ You also teach, 'If someone swears by the altar, he isn't bound by his vow; but if he swears by the gift on the altar, he is bound.' ¹⁹ How blind you are! Which is the more important, the gift or the altar which makes the gift holy? ²⁰ So then, when a person swears by the altar, he is swearing by it and by all the gifts on it; ²¹ and when he swears by the Temple, he is swearing by it and by God, who lives there; ²² and when someone swears by heaven, he is swearing by God's throne and by him who sits on it.

²³ "How terrible for you, teachers of the Law and Pharisees! You hypocrites! You give to God a tenth even of the seasoning herbs, such as mint, dill, and cumin, but you

neglect to obey the really important teachings of the Law, such as justice and mercy and honesty. These you should practise, without neglecting the others. ²⁴ Blind guides! You strain a fly out of your drink, but swallow a camel!

²⁵ "How terrible for you, teachers of the Law and Pharisees! You hypocrites! You clean the outside of your cup and plate, while the inside is full of what you have obtained by violence and selfishness. ²⁶ Blind Pharisee! Clean what is inside the cup first, and then the outside will be clean too!

²⁷ "How terrible for you, teachers of the Law and Pharisees! You hypocrites! You are like whitewashed tombs, which look fine on the outside but are full of bones and decaying corpses on the inside. ²⁸ In the same way, on the outside you appear good to everybody, but inside you are full of hypocrisy and sins.

Jesus Predicts their Punishment
(Lk 11.47–51)

²⁹ "How terrible for you, teachers of the Law and Pharisees! You hypocrites! You make fine tombs for the prophets and decorate the monuments of those who lived good lives; ³⁰ and you claim that if you had lived during the time of your ancestors, you would not have done what they did and killed the prophets. ³¹ So you actually admit that you are the descendants of those who murdered the prophets! ³² Go on, then, and finish what your ancestors started! ³³ You snakes and children of snakes! How do you expect to escape from being condemned to hell? ³⁴ And so I tell you that I will send you prophets and wise men and teachers; you will kill some of them, crucify others, and whip others in the synagogues and chase them from town to town. ³⁵ As a result, the punishment for the murder of all innocent people will fall on you, from the murder of innocent Abel to the murder of Zachariah son of Berachiah, whom you murdered between the Temple and the altar. ³⁶ I tell you indeed: the punishment for all these murders will fall on the people of this day!

Jesus' Love for Jerusalem
(Lk 13.34–35)

³⁷ "Jerusalem, Jerusalem! You kill the prophets and stone the messengers God has sent you! How many times have I wanted to put my arms round all your people, just as a hen gathers her chicks under her wings, but you would not let me! ³⁸ And so your Temple will be abandoned and empty. ³⁹ From now on, I tell you, you will never see me again until you say, 'God bless him who comes in the name of the Lord.' "

Jesus Speaks of the Destruction of the Temple
(Mk 13.1–2; Lk 21.5–6)

24 Jesus left and was going away from the Temple when his disciples came to him to call his attention to its buildings. ² "Yes," he said, "you may well look at all these. I tell you this: not a single stone here will be left in its place; every one of them will be thrown down."

Troubles and Persecutions
(Mk 13.3–13; Lk 21.7–19)

³ As Jesus sat on the Mount of Olives, the disciples came to him in private. "Tell us when all this will be," they asked, "and what will happen to show that it is the time for your coming and the end of the age."

⁴ Jesus answered, "Be on your guard, and do not let anyone deceive you. ⁵ Many men, claiming to speak for me, will come and say, 'I am the Messiah!' and they will deceive many people. ⁶ You are going to hear the noise of battles close by and the news of battles far away; but do not be troubled. Such things must happen, but they do not mean that the end has come. ⁷ Countries will fight each other, kingdoms will attack one another. There will be famines and earthquakes everywhere. ⁸ All these things are like the first pains of childbirth.

⁹ "Then you will be arrested and handed over to be punished and be put to death. All nations will hate you because of me. ¹⁰ Many will give up their faith at that time; they will betray one another and hate one another. ¹¹ Then many false prophets will appear and deceive many people.

¹² Such will be the spread of evil that many people's love will grow cold. ¹³ But whoever holds out to the end will be saved. ¹⁴ And this Good News about the Kingdom will be preached through all the world for a witness to all nations; and then the end will come.

The Awful Horror
(Mk 13.14–23; Lk 21.20–24)

¹⁵ "You will see 'The Awful Horror' of which the prophet Daniel spoke. It will be standing in the holy place." (Note to the reader: be sure to understand what this means!) ¹⁶ "Then those who are in Judea must run away to the hills. ¹⁷ Someone who is on the roof of his house must not take the time to go down and get his belongings from the house. ¹⁸ Someone who is in the field must not go back to get his cloak. ¹⁹ How terrible it will be in those days for women who are pregnant and for mothers with little babies! ²⁰ Pray to God that you will not have to run away during the winter or on a Sabbath! ²¹ For the trouble at that time will be far more terrible than any there has ever been, from the beginning of the world to this very day. Nor will there ever be anything like it again. ²² But God has already reduced the number of days; had he not done so, nobody would survive. For the sake of his chosen people, however, God will reduce the days.

²³ "Then, if anyone says to you, 'Look, here is the Messiah!' or 'There he is!' — do not believe it. ²⁴ For false Messiahs and false prophets will appear; they will perform great miracles and wonders in order to deceive even God's chosen people, if possible. ²⁵ Listen! I have told you this before the time comes.

²⁶ "Or, if people should tell you, 'Look, he is out in the desert!' — don't go there; or if they say, 'Look, he is hiding here!' — don't believe it. ²⁷ For the Son of Man will come like the lightning which flashes across the whole sky from the east to the west.

²⁸ "Wherever there is a dead body, the vultures will gather.

The Coming of the Son of Man
(Mk 13.24–27; Lk 21.25–28)

[29] "Soon after the trouble of those days, the sun will grow dark, the moon will no longer shine, the stars will fall from heaven, and the powers in space will be driven from their courses. [30] Then the sign of the Son of Man will appear in the sky; and all the peoples of earth will weep as they see the Son of Man coming on the clouds of heaven with power and great glory. [31] The great trumpet will sound, and he will send out his angels to the four corners of the earth, and they will gather his chosen people from one end of the world to the other.

The Lesson of the Fig Tree
(Mk 13.28–31; Lk 21.29–33)

[32] "Let the fig tree teach you a lesson. When its branches become green and tender and it starts putting out leaves, you know that summer is near. [33] In the same way, when you see all these things, you will know that the time is near, ready to begin. [a] [34] Remember that all these things will happen before the people now living have all died. [35] Heaven and earth will pass away, but my words will never pass away.

No One Knows the Day and Hour
(Mk 13.32–37; Lk 17.26–30, 34–36)

[36] "No one knows, however, when that day and hour will come — neither the angels in heaven nor the Son; [b] the Father alone knows. [37] The coming of the Son of Man will be like what happened in the time of Noah. [38] In the days before the flood people ate and drank, men and women married, up to the very day Noah went into the boat; [39] yet they did not realize what was happening until the flood came and swept them all away. That is how it will be when the Son of Man comes. [40] At that time two men will be working in a field: one will be taken away, the other will be left behind. [41] Two women will be at a mill grinding meal: one will be taken away, the other will be left behind.

[42] "Be on your guard, then, because you do not know what day your Lord will come. [43] If the owner of a house knew the

a **24.33** the time is near, ready to begin; *or* he is near, ready to come.
b **24.36** *Some manuscripts do not have* nor the Son.

time when the thief would come, you can be sure that he would stay awake and not let the thief break into his house. [44] So then, you also must always be ready, because the Son of Man will come at an hour when you are not expecting him.

The Faithful or the Unfaithful Servant
(Lk 12.41–48)

[45] "Who, then, is a faithful and wise servant? It is the one that his master has placed in charge of the other servants to give them their food at the proper time. [46] How happy that servant is if his master finds him doing this when he comes home! [47] Indeed, I tell you, the master will put that servant in charge of all his property. [48] But if he is a bad servant, he will tell himself that his master will not come back for a long time, [49] and he will begin to beat his fellow-servants and to eat and drink with drunkards. [50] Then that servant's master will come back one day when the servant does not expect him and at a time he does not know. [51] The master will cut him in pieces[a] and make him share the fate of the hypocrites. There he will cry and grind his teeth.

The Parable of the Ten Young Women

25 "At that time the Kingdom of heaven will be like this. Once there were ten young women who took their oil lamps and went out to meet the bridegroom. [2] Five of them were foolish, and the other five were wise. [3] The foolish ones took their lamps but did not take any extra oil with them, [4] while the wise ones took containers full of oil for their lamps. [5] The bridegroom was late in coming, so the women began to nod and fall asleep.

[6] "It was already midnight when the cry rang out, 'Here is the bridegroom! Come and meet him!' [7] The ten women woke up and trimmed their lamps. [8] Then the foolish ones said to the wise ones, 'Let us have some of your oil, because our lamps are going out.' [9] 'No, indeed,' the wise ones answered, 'there is not enough for you and for us. Go to the shop and buy some for yourselves.' [10] So the foolish women went off to buy some oil; and while they were gone, the

a **24.51** cut him in pieces; or throw him out.

bridegroom arrived. The five who were ready went in with him to the wedding feast, and the door was closed.

¹¹ "Later the other women arrived. 'Sir, sir! Let us in!' they cried out. ¹² 'Certainly not! I don't know you,' the bridegroom answered."

¹³ And Jesus concluded, "Be on your guard, then, because you do not know the day or the hour.

The Parable of the Three Servants
(Lk 19.11–27)

¹⁴ "At that time the Kingdom of heaven will be like this. Once there was a man who was about to go on a journey; he called his servants and put them in charge of his property. ¹⁵ He gave to each one according to his ability: to one he gave five thousand gold coins, to another he gave two thousand, and to another he gave one thousand. Then he left on his journey. ¹⁶ The servant who had received five thousand coins went at once and invested his money and earned another five thousand. ¹⁷ In the same way the servant who had received two thousand coins earned another two thousand. ¹⁸ But the servant who had received one thousand coins went off, dug a hole in the ground, and hid his master's money.

¹⁹ "After a long time the master of those servants came back and settled accounts with them. ²⁰ The servant who had received five thousand coins came in and handed over the other five thousand. 'You gave me five thousand coins, sir,' he said. 'Look! Here are another five thousand that I have earned.' ²¹ 'Well done, you good and faithful servant!' said his master. 'You have been faithful in managing small amounts, so I will put you in charge of large amounts. Come on in and share my happiness!'

²² "Then the servant who had been given two thousand coins came in and said, 'You gave me two thousand coins, sir. Look! Here are another two thousand that I have earned.' ²³ 'Well done, you good and faithful servant!' said his master. 'You have been faithful in managing small amounts, so I will put you in charge of large amounts. Come on in and share my happiness!'

²⁴ "Then the servant who had received one thousand coins came in and said, 'Sir, I know you are a hard man; you reap harvests where you did not sow, and you gather crops where you did not scatter seed. ²⁵ I was afraid, so I went off and hid your money in the ground. Look! Here is what belongs to you.'

²⁶ " 'You bad and lazy servant!' his master said. 'You knew, did you, that I reap harvests where I did not sow, and gather crops where I did not scatter seed? ²⁷ Well, then, you should have deposited my money in the bank, and I would have received it all back with interest when I returned. ²⁸ Now, take the money away from him and give it to the one who has ten thousand coins. ²⁹ For to every person who has something, even more will be given, and he will have more than enough; but the person who has nothing, even the little that he has will be taken away from him. ³⁰ As for this useless servant — throw him outside in the darkness; there he will cry and grind his teeth.'

The Final Judgement

³¹ "When the Son of Man comes as King and all the angels with him, he will sit on his royal throne, ³² and the people of all the nations will be gathered before him. Then he will divide them into two groups, just as a shepherd separates the sheep from the goats. ³³ He will put the righteous people on his right and the others on his left. ³⁴ Then the King will say to the people on his right, 'Come, you that are blessed by my Father! Come and possess the kingdom which has been prepared for you ever since the creation of the world. ³⁵ I was hungry and you fed me, thirsty and you gave me a drink; I was a stranger and you received me in your homes, ³⁶ naked and you clothed me; I was sick and you took care of me, in prison and you visited me.'

³⁷ "The righteous will then answer him, 'When, Lord, did we ever see you hungry and feed you, or thirsty and give you a drink? ³⁸ When did we ever see you a stranger and welcome you in our homes, or naked and clothe you? ³⁹ When did we ever see you sick or in prison, and visit you?' ⁴⁰ The King will reply, 'I tell you, whenever you did this for one of the least important of these members of my family, you did it for me!'

⁴¹ "Then he will say to those on his left, 'Away from me, you that are under God's curse! Away to the eternal fire which has been prepared for the Devil and his angels! ⁴²I was hungry but you would not feed me, thirsty but you would not give me a drink; ⁴³ I was a stranger but you would not welcome me in your homes, naked but you would not clothe me; I was sick and in prison but you would not take care of me.'

⁴⁴ "Then they will answer him, 'When, Lord, did we ever see you hungry or thirsty or a stranger or naked or sick or in prison, and would not help you?' ⁴⁵ The King will reply, 'I tell you, whenever you refused to help one of these least important ones, you refused to help me.' ⁴⁶ These, then, will be sent off to eternal punishment, but the righteous will go to eternal life."

The Plot against Jesus
(Mk 14.1–2; Lk 22.1–2; Jn 11.45–53)

26 When Jesus had finished teaching all these things, he said to his disciples, ² "In two days, as you know, it will be the Passover Festival, and the Son of Man will be handed over to be crucified."

³ Then the chief priests and the elders met together in the palace of Caiaphas, the High Priest, ⁴ and made plans to arrest Jesus secretly and put him to death. ⁵ "We must not do it during the festival," they said, "or the people will riot."

Jesus is Anointed at Bethany
(Mk 14.3–9; Jn 12.1–8)

⁶ Jesus was in Bethany at the house of Simon, a man who had suffered from a dreaded skin disease. ⁷ While Jesus was eating, a woman came to him with an alabaster jar filled with an expensive perfume, which she poured on his head. ⁸ The disciples saw this and became angry. "Why all this waste?" they asked. ⁹ "This perfume could have been sold for a large amount and the money given to the poor!"

¹⁰ Jesus knew what they were saying, so he said to them, "Why are you bothering this woman? It is a fine and beautiful thing that she has done for me. ¹¹ You will always have poor people with you, but you will not always have me. ¹² What she did was to pour this perfume on my body to get me ready for

burial. [13]Now, I assure you that wherever this gospel is preached all over the world, what she has done will be told in memory of her."

Judas Agrees to Betray Jesus
(Mk 14.10–11; Lk 22.3–6)

[14]Then one of the twelve disciples — the one named Judas Iscariot — went to the chief priests [15]and asked, "What will you give me if I betray Jesus to you?" They counted out 30 silver coins and gave them to him. [16]From then on Judas was looking for a good chance to hand Jesus over to them.

The disciples ... prepared the Passover meal.   (26.19)

Jesus Eats the Passover Meal with his Disciples
(Mk 14.12–21; Lk 22.7–13, 21–23; Jn 13.21–30)

[17]On the first day of the Festival of Unleavened Bread the disciples came to Jesus and asked him, "Where do you want us to get the Passover meal ready for you?"

[18]"Go to a certain man in the city," he said to them, "and tell him: 'The Teacher says, My hour has come; my disciples and I will celebrate the Passover at your house.' "

[19]The disciples did as Jesus had told them and prepared the Passover meal.

[20]When it was evening, Jesus and the twelve disciples sat down to eat. [21]During the meal Jesus said, "I tell you, one of you will betray me."

[22] The disciples were very upset and began to ask him, one after the other, "Surely, Lord, you don't mean me?"

[23] Jesus answered, "One who dips his bread in the dish with me will betray me. [24] The Son of Man will die as the Scriptures say he will, but how terrible for that man who betrays the Son of Man! It would have been better for that man if he had never been born!"

[25] Judas, the traitor, spoke up. "Surely, Teacher, you don't mean me?" he asked.

Jesus answered, "So you say."

The Lord's Supper
(Mk 14.22–26; Lk 22.14–20; 1 Cor. 11.23–25)

[26] While they were eating, Jesus took a piece of bread, gave a prayer of thanks, broke it, and gave it to his disciples. "Take and eat it," he said; "this is my body."

[27] Then he took a cup, gave thanks to God, and gave it to them. "Drink it, all of you," he said; [28] "this is my blood, which seals God's covenant, my blood poured out for many for the forgiveness of sins. [29] I tell you, I will never again drink this wine until the day I drink the new wine with you in my Father's Kingdom."

[30] Then they sang a hymn and went out to the Mount of Olives.

Jesus Predicts Peter's Denial
(Mk 14.27–31; Lk 22.31–34; Jn 13.36–38)

[31] Then Jesus said to them, "This very night all of you will run away and leave me, for the scripture says, 'God will kill the shepherd, and the sheep of the flock will be scattered.' [32] But after I am raised to life, I will go to Galilee ahead of you."

[33] Peter spoke up and said to Jesus, "I will never leave you, even though all the rest do!"

[34] Jesus said to Peter, "I tell you that before the cock crows tonight, you will say three times that you do not know me."

[35] Peter answered, "I will never say that, even if I have to die with you!"

And all the other disciples said the same thing.

Jesus Prays in Gethsemane
(Mk 14.32–42; Lk 22.39–46)

³⁶Then Jesus went with his disciples to a place called Gethsemane, and he said to them, "Sit here while I go over there and pray." ³⁷He took with him Peter and the two sons of Zebedee. Grief and anguish came over him, ³⁸and he said to them, "The sorrow in my heart is so great that it almost crushes me. Stay here and keep watch with me."

³⁹He went a little farther on, threw himself face downwards on the ground, and prayed, "My Father, if it is possible, take this cup of suffering from me! Yet not what I want, but what you want."

... *before the cock crows* ...   (26.34)

⁴⁰Then he returned to the three disciples and found them asleep; and he said to Peter, "How is it that you three were not able to keep watch with me even for one hour? ⁴¹Keep watch and pray that you will not fall into temptation. The spirit is willing, but the flesh is weak."

⁴²Once more Jesus went away and prayed, "My Father, if this cup of suffering cannot be taken away unless I drink it, your will be done." ⁴³He returned once more and found the disciples asleep; they could not keep their eyes open.

⁴⁴Again Jesus left them, went away, and prayed the third time, saying the same words. ⁴⁵Then he returned to the disciples and said, "Are you still sleeping and resting? Look! The hour has come for the Son of Man to be handed over to the power of sinners. ⁴⁶Get up, let us go. Look, here is the man who is betraying me!"

The Arrest of Jesus
(Mk 14.43–50; Lk 22.47–53; Jn 18.3–12)

[47] Jesus was still speaking when Judas, one of the twelve disciples, arrived. With him was a large crowd armed with swords and clubs and sent by the chief priests and the elders. [48] The traitor had given the crowd a signal: "The man I kiss is the one you want. Arrest him!"

[49] Judas went straight to Jesus and said, "Peace be with you, Teacher," and kissed him.

[50] Jesus answered, "Be quick about it, friend!" [a]

Then they came up, arrested Jesus, and held him tight. [51] One of those who were with Jesus drew his sword and struck at the High Priest's slave, cutting off his ear. [52] "Put your sword back in its place," Jesus said to him. "All who take the sword will die by the sword. [53] Don't you know that I could call on my Father for help, and at once he would send me more than twelve armies of angels? [54] But in that case, how could the Scriptures come true which say that this is what must happen?"

[55] Then Jesus spoke to the crowd, "Did you have to come with swords and clubs to capture me, as though I were an outlaw? Every day I sat down and taught in the Temple, and you did not arrest me. [56] But all this has happened in order to make what the prophets wrote in the Scriptures come true."

Then all the disciples left him and ran away.

Jesus Before the Council
(Mk 14.53–65; Lk 22.54–55, 63–71; Jn 18.13–14, 19–24)

[57] Those who had arrested Jesus took him to the house of Caiaphas, the High Priest, where the teachers of the Law and the elders had gathered together. [58] Peter followed from a distance, as far as the courtyard of the High Priest's house. He went into the courtyard and sat down with the guards to see how it would all come out. [59] The chief priests and the whole Council tried to find some false evidence against Jesus to put him to death; [60] but they could not find any, even though many people came forward and told lies about him.

a **26.50** Be quick about it, friend!; *or* Why are you here, friend?

Finally two men stepped up [61] and said, "This man said, 'I am able to tear down God's Temple and three days later build it up again.' "

[62] The High Priest stood up and said to Jesus, "Have you no answer to give to this accusation against you?" [63] But Jesus kept quiet. Again the High Priest spoke to him, "In the name of the living God I now put you on oath: tell us if you are the Messiah, the Son of God."

[64] Jesus answered him, "So you say. But I tell all of you: from this time on you will see the Son of Man sitting on the right of the Almighty and coming on the clouds of heaven!"

[65] At this the High Priest tore his clothes and said, "Blasphemy! We don't need any more witnesses! You have just heard his blasphemy! [66] What do you think?"

They answered, "He is guilty and must die."

[67] Then they spat in his face and beat him; and those who slapped him [68] said, "Prophesy for us, Messiah! Guess who hit you!"

Peter Denies Jesus
(Mk 14.66–72; Lk 22.56–62; Jn 18.15–18, 25–27)

[69] Peter was sitting outside in the courtyard when one of the High Priest's servant women came to him and said, "You, too, were with Jesus of Galilee."

[70] But he denied it in front of them all. "I don't know what you are talking about," he answered, [71] and went on out to the entrance of the courtyard. Another servant woman saw him and said to the men there, "He was with Jesus of Nazareth."

[72] Again Peter denied it and answered, "I swear that I don't know that man!"

[73] After a little while the men standing there came to Peter. "Of course you are one of them," they said. "After all, the way you speak gives you away!"

[74] Then Peter said, "I swear that I am telling the truth! May God punish me if I am not! I do not know that man!"

Just then a cock crowed, [75] and Peter remembered what Jesus had told him: "Before the cock crows, you will say three times that you do not know me." He went out and wept bitterly.

Jesus is Taken to Pilate
(Mk 15.1; Lk 23.1–2; Jn 18.28–32)

27 Early in the morning all the chief priests and the
elders made their plans against Jesus to put him to
death. ² They put him in chains, led him off, and handed him
over to Pilate, the Roman governor.

The Death of Judas
(Acts 1.18–19)

³ When Judas, the traitor, learnt that Jesus had been
condemned, he repented and took back the 30 silver coins to
the chief priests and the elders. ⁴ "I have sinned by betraying
an innocent man to death!" he said.

"What do we care about that?" they answered. "That is
your business!"

⁵ Judas threw the coins down in the Temple and left; then
he went off and hanged himself.

⁶ The chief priests picked up the coins and said, "This is
blood money, and it is against our Law to put it in the temple
treasury." ⁷ After reaching an agreement about it, they used
the money to buy Potter's Field, as a cemetery for foreigners.
⁸ That is why that field is called "Field of Blood" to this very
day.

⁹ Then what the prophet Jeremiah had said came true:
"They took the thirty silver coins, the amount the people of
Israel had agreed to pay for him, ¹⁰ and used the money to
buy the potter's field, as the Lord had commanded me."

Pilate Questions Jesus
(Mk 15.2–5; Lk 23.3–5; Jn 18.33–38)

¹¹ Jesus stood before the Roman governor, who ques-
tioned him. "Are you the king of the Jews?" he asked.

"So you say," answered Jesus. ¹² But he said nothing in
response to the accusations of the chief priests and elders.

¹³ So Pilate said to him, "Don't you hear all these things
they accuse you of?"

¹⁴ But Jesus refused to answer a single word, with the result
that the Governor was greatly surprised.

Jesus is Sentenced to Death
(Mk 15.6–15; Lk 23.13–25; Jn 18.39—19.16)

[15] At every Passover Festival the Roman governor was in the habit of setting free any one prisoner the crowd asked for. [16] At that time there was a well-known prisoner named Jesus Barabbas. [17] So when the crowd gathered, Pilate asked them, "Which one do you want me to set free for you? Jesus Barabbas or Jesus called the Messiah?" [18] He knew very well that the Jewish authorities had handed Jesus over to him because they were jealous.

[19] While Pilate was sitting in the judgement hall, his wife sent him a message: "Have nothing to do with that innocent man, because in a dream last night I suffered much on account of him."

[20] The chief priests and the elders persuaded the crowd to ask Pilate to set Barabbas free and have Jesus put to death. [21] But Pilate asked the crowd, "Which one of these two do you want me to set free for you?"

"Barabbas!" they answered.

[22] "What, then, shall I do with Jesus called the Messiah?" Pilate asked them.

"Crucify him!" they all answered.

[23] But Pilate asked, "What crime has he committed?"

Then they started shouting at the top of their voices: "Crucify him!"

[24] When Pilate saw that it was no use to go on, but that a riot might break out, he took some water, washed his hands in front of the crowd, and said, "I am not responsible for the death of this man! This is your doing!"

[25] The whole crowd answered, "Let the responsibility for his death fall on us and our children!"

[26] Then Pilate set Barabbas free for them; and after he had Jesus whipped, he handed him over to be crucified.

The Soldiers Mock Jesus
(Mk 15.16–20; Jn 19.2–3)

[27] Then Pilate's soldiers took Jesus into the governor's palace, and the whole company gathered round him. [28] They stripped off his clothes and put a scarlet robe on

him. ²⁹ Then they made a crown out of thorny branches and placed it on his head, and put a stick in his right hand; then they knelt before him and mocked him. "Long live the King of the Jews!" they said. ³⁰ They spat on him, and took the stick and hit him over the head. ³¹ When they had finished mocking him, they took the robe off and put his own clothes back on him. Then they led him out to crucify him.

Jesus is Crucified
(Mk 15.21–32; Lk 23.26–43; Jn 19.17–27)

³² As they were going out, they met a man from Cyrene named Simon, and the soldiers forced him to carry Jesus' cross. ³³ They came to a place called Golgotha, which means, "The Place of the Skull". ³⁴ There they offered Jesus wine mixed with a bitter substance; but after tasting it, he would not drink it.

³⁵ They crucified him and then divided his clothes among them by throwing dice. ³⁶ After that they sat there and watched him. ³⁷ Above his head they put the written notice of the accusation against him: "This is Jesus, the King of the Jews." ³⁸ Then they crucified two bandits with Jesus, one on his right and the other on his left.

³⁹ People passing by shook their heads and hurled insults at Jesus: ⁴⁰ "You were going to tear down the Temple and build it up again in three days! Save yourself if you are God's Son! Come on down from the cross!"

⁴¹ In the same way the chief priests and the teachers of the Law and the elders jeered at him: ⁴² "He saved others, but he cannot save himself! Isn't he the king of Israel? If he comes down off the cross now, we will believe in him! ⁴³ He trusts in God and claims to be God's Son. Well, then, let us see if God wants to save him now!"

⁴⁴ Even the bandits who had been crucified with him insulted him in the same way.

The Death of Jesus
(Mk 15.33–41; Lk 23.44–49; Jn 19.28–30)

⁴⁵ At noon the whole country was covered with darkness, which lasted for three hours. ⁴⁶ At about three o'clock

Jesus cried out with a loud shout, "*Eli, Eli, lema sabachthani?*" which means, "My God, my God, why did you abandon me?"

⁴⁷ Some of the people standing there heard him and said, "He is calling for Elijah!" ⁴⁸ One of them ran up at once, took a sponge, soaked it in cheap wine, put it on the end of a stick, and tried to make him drink it.

⁴⁹ But the others said, "Wait, let us see if Elijah is coming to save him!"

⁵⁰ Jesus again gave a loud cry and breathed his last.

⁵¹ Then the curtain hanging in the Temple was torn in two from top to bottom. The earth shook, the rocks split apart, ⁵² the graves broke open, and many of God's people who had died were raised to life. ⁵³ They left the graves, and after Jesus rose from death, they went into the Holy City, where many people saw them.

⁵⁴ When the army officer and the soldiers with him who were watching Jesus saw the earthquake and everything else that happened, they were terrified and said, "He really was the Son of God!"

⁵⁵ There were many women there, looking on from a distance, who had followed Jesus from Galilee and helped him. ⁵⁶ Among them were Mary Magdalene, Mary the mother of James and Joseph, and the wife of Zebedee.

The Burial of Jesus
(Mk 15.42–47; Lk 23.50–56; Jn 19.38–42)

⁵⁷ When it was evening, a rich man from Arimathea arrived; his name was Joseph, and he also was a disciple of Jesus. ⁵⁸ He went into the presence of Pilate and asked for the body of Jesus. Pilate gave orders for the body to be given to Joseph. ⁵⁹ So Joseph took it, wrapped it in a new linen sheet, ⁶⁰ and placed it in his own tomb, which he had just recently dug out of solid rock. Then he rolled a large stone across the entrance to the tomb and went away. ⁶¹ Mary Magdalene and the other Mary were sitting there, facing the tomb.

The Guard at the Tomb

⁶² The next day, which was a Sabbath, the chief priests and the Pharisees met with Pilate ⁶³ and said, "Sir, we remember that while that liar was still alive he said, 'I will be raised to life three days later.' ⁶⁴ Give orders, then, for his tomb to be carefully guarded until the third day, so that his disciples will not be able to go and steal the body, and then tell the people that he was raised from death. This last lie would be even worse than the first one."

⁶⁵ "Take a guard," Pilate told them; "go and make the tomb as secure as you can."

⁶⁶ So they left and made the tomb secure by putting a seal on the stone and leaving the guard on watch.

The Resurrection
(Mk 16.1–10; Lk 24.1–12; Jn 20.1–10)

28 After the Sabbath, as Sunday morning was dawning, Mary Magdalene and the other Mary went to look at the tomb. ² Suddenly there was a violent earthquake; an angel of the Lord came down from heaven, rolled the stone away, and sat on it. ³ His appearance was like lightning, and his clothes were white as snow. ⁴ The guards were so afraid that they trembled and became like dead men.

⁵ The angel spoke to the women. "You must not be afraid," he said. "I know you are looking for Jesus, who was crucified. ⁶ He is not here; he has been raised, just as he said. Come here and see the place where he was lying. ⁷ Go quickly now, and tell his disciples, 'He has been raised from death, and now he is going to Galilee ahead of you; there you will see him!' Remember what I have told you."

⁸ So they left the tomb in a hurry, afraid and yet filled with joy, and ran to tell his disciples.

⁹ Suddenly Jesus met them and said, "Peace be with you." They came up to him, took hold of his feet, and worshipped him. ¹⁰ "Do not be afraid," Jesus said to them. "Go and tell my brothers to go to Galilee, and there they will see me."

The Report of the Guard

[11] While the women went on their way, some of the soldiers guarding the tomb went back to the city and told the chief priests everything that had happened. [12] The chief priests met with the elders and made their plan; they gave a large sum of money to the soldiers [13] and said, "You are to say that his disciples came during the night and stole his body while you were asleep. [14] And if the Governor should hear of this, we will convince him that you are innocent, and you will have nothing to worry about."

[15] The guards took the money and did what they were told to do. And so that is the report spread round by the Jews to this very day.

Jesus Appears to his Disciples
(Mk 16.14–18; Lk 24.36–49; Jn 20.19–23; Acts 1.6–8)

[16] The eleven disciples went to the hill in Galilee where Jesus had told them to go. [17] When they saw him, they worshipped him, even though some of them doubted. [18] Jesus drew near and said to them, "I have been given all authority in heaven and on earth. [19] Go, then, to all peoples everywhere and make them my disciples: baptize them in the name of the Father, the Son, and the Holy Spirit, [20] and teach them to obey everything I have commanded you. And I will be with you always, to the end of the age."

PALESTINE
IN THE TIME OF
JESUS

MEDITERRANEAN SEA

Sidon

Zarephath

Tyre

PHOENICIA

ITUREA

ABILENE

Caesarea
Philippi

GALILEE

Chorazin
Capernaum
Cana
Tiberias
Nazareth
Nain

TRACHONITIS

Bethsaida

LAKE GALILEE

Gadara

D
E
C
A
P
O
L
I
S
(THE TEN TOWNS)

Mount
Carmel

Caesarea

Salim
Aenon

Gerasa

Mount Gerizim
Sychar

SAMARIA

Arimathea

Ephraim

Jericho

Emmaus

Jerusalem
Bethphage
Bethany
Qumran
Bethlehem

JUDEA

PEREA

River Jordan

DEAD SEA

IDUMEA

0   20   40   60

Kilometres

82

**JERUSALEM IN
NEW TESTAMENT TIMES**

To Caesarea

Present City Wall

To Jericho

Damascus
Gate

Pool of
Bethzatha

PRAETORIUM

Ancient
City Wall

FORT

Gate

TEMPLE

To Bethany

Golgotha

Gethsemane

Gate

Beautiful Gate

To Joppa

Gate

Court of
Gentiles

Solomon's
Porch

Gennath
Gate

Bridge

Gates

To Bethlehem

HEROD'S
PALACE

KIDRON VALLEY

Pool

Present City Wall

Pool of
Siloam

| 0 | 200 | 400 |

Metres

Gate

Roads

To Dead
Sea

VALLEY OF HINNOM

WHERE TO LOOK WHEN YOU ARE FEELING ...

SCRIPTURE UNION READING HELPS GUIDE

Scripture Union Scotland offers a selection of products to help you read your Bible.

If you are 7 or 8, try the new *'Let's Go'*. *'Let's Go'* takes you travelling through time to revisit Bible scenes, bringing people and places to life.

For 9s to 11s *'Check it Out!'* is designed to fit into a mini-binder divided by subject, including diary pages, puzzles, and true stories. The Bible story is the focus each week for a variety of activities.

'One Up' is for young teens. Daily Bible readings to change your life. *'One Up'* deals with issues facing teenagers today. This is a must for 11s to 14s.

'Daily Bread' is for adults to use who want a practical guide to Bible reading.

'Alive to God' is an alternative for adults which encourages imaginative, thoughtful and reflective responses to the Bible.

'Encounter With God', also for adults, is designed to encourage an in-depth approach to systematic Bible reading.

NOTES

NOTES

NOTES

NOTES

Good News New Testament – Second Edition © 1994

Text, illustrations and all helps are copyright
New Testament © American Bible Society 1966, 1971, 1976, 1992
Maps © United Bible Societies 1976, 1978

Title	Code	ISBN
Gospel of Matthew	GNB560P MT	0 901518 20 4

1996/50M

Quotation Rights for the Good News Bible